East meets West

in Aloka's Kitchen

by Aloka Ray

Best wishes
Aloka Ray

This book is dedicated to my parents,
who have always inspired me in all my creations;
and to my children, Mimi and Jojo,
who I hope will enjoy making the recipes
in their kitchens in the future.

East meets West in Aloka's Kitchen
by Aloka Ray

First published 2014
by Close Publications
Wells, Somerset, UK

Design by Iain MacLeod-Jones and Tim Wood
www.imjdesign.co.uk

Food photography by Sandeep Ray
Cover photography and author photographs by Iain MacLeod-Jones

Print production by St Andrews Press, Wells, Somerset
www.standrewspress.co.uk

Contents

Introduction

Dear Readers,

Cooking has always been my passion since I was in my teens. I owe my love of cooking primarily to my mother and my aunt. I remember admiring their cooking skills as a child and I would wait patiently for my turn in the kitchen after they had finished. Over the years my interest in cooking developed to the point that I started experimenting with food and coming up with new dishes. I participated in some food festivals in India and won a few prizes for my creations too.

My husband, children and their cousins, Esha and Ryan, have always enjoyed the food I cook for them. When I moved to England ten years ago, I often invited my friends over for lunch and they too simply loved the curries that I made for them. My dear friend Berit Lindholm was always full of appreciation. It was she who asked me to teach my friends the art of Indian cooking because she said my recipes were not only healthy and tasty but easy to make too. Inspired by her constant encouragement I decided to take a few classes and a couple of months later I shared my special recipes in a class named 'Aloka's Kitchen'.

My friends were so impressed with the delicious recipes that they encouraged me to publish a book. 'East meets West' is my first cookery book in which I have shared some very interesting and tasty recipes.

Most of the dishes are not hot as the addition of chillies is optional in most cases. However, if you do like your curries hot and spicy, you may add more chillies according to taste. The ingredients used are not only fresh but they have some beneficial health properties too, as long as the oil and salt is used at an optimum level.

I sincerely hope that you will enjoy making the curries at home and your encouragement will inspire me to bring out more editions of this book in future.

Aloka Ray

I am delighted to have been able to attend several of Aloka's cooking classes. I am not a great cook and have been amazed that I have been able to put together a great meal, let alone an Indian meal! Aloka is an amazing teacher, she breaks it down for everyone to understand clearly, and for everyone to be able to make it at home too. She always explains when substitutions are possible, so the recipes are absolutely suitable for anyone. I would be thrilled if her recipes would appear in a book; it will bridge the gap for many of us who are initially apprehensive about Indian cooking and I am sure it will bring joy to many a family!

Rixt Hiemstra (Works at 'Disney on Ice')

I have been trying to cook curries for years, but the wonderful fragrances of the spices are usually overwhelmed by the heat of the chilli or combine to produce an unappetising meal. Most recipes seem to use ingredients which are unavailable locally or methods which are very complex and time consuming. With some regret I had reverted to the familiar tried and tested British cooking, until I was introduced to Aloka's Indian family cooking. Aloka has simplified her recipes so even a novice can produce a successful result. I have cooked her dishes for friends and family and they have been received with enthusiasm, even by the younger members; the chicken and cashew in particular has become a firm favourite. One great bonus with these recipes is that Aloka explains when substitutions can be made if ingredients are unavailable and encourages the cook to make small alterations according to individual taste. I have tried all the recipes and the results are reliable, simple, and are not only mouth-wateringly aromatic but also delicious. I wish her the greatest success with her book and I'm sure will be a popular read with many enthusiastic family cooks.

Madeleine (Occupational therapist)

I love curries but have never been able to make a good curry sauce, so most of my efforts have been very mediocre. Aloka's recipes have opened my eyes to how simple preparing curry can be. The recipes are mild and easy to follow and you can alter them to your personal taste. I particularly like the slow-cooked lamb curry and the cashew chicken curry. My wife was quite impressed by my humble efforts!

Terry Ricketts (Driving Instructor)

Useful Cooking Tips

in Indian Cooking

1 Most of the spices, paneer and chappatis are available in Asian supermarkets. I usually buy my spices from Tesco and paneer from Waitrose.

2 It will be very useful to buy a measuring cup which will help you to measure the amount of water and cream accurately.

3 Chillies and chilli powder are hot so use them only if you like your food hot and spicy.

4 Just to let you know that tsp stands for teaspoon and tbsp stands for tablespoon. Always wash coriander thoroughly before use.

5 Indian cooking requires water in several dishes. It is up to you how much sauce or gravy you require so you may have to adjust the water accordingly. I have given approximate water measurements but you may need to add more water if you require. On the other hand, if the sauce is too thin, you may have to keep it longer on the hob until it attains the right consistency.

6 Keeping the pan half covered during cooking will help to bring a beautiful colour to the dish. If you cover it completely, the colour is often lost during cooking.

7 Since a lot of the dishes involve frying, it is best to lower the heat and then add the ingredients carefully to keep the spluttering to a minimum.

8 Paneer is an Indian cheese and is a great source of protein for vegetarians.

9 Using a non-stick pan always helps if you're weight watching as you can use less oil.

10 Indian curries taste good with salt but the amount of salt and oil you use is totally up to your taste and preferences.

11 Certain dishes that contain dairy products or nuts may be quite filling, so it is advisable to have a light dessert for easy digestion.

Yellow Lentil Bhajis

Serves 6-8

250g of yellow split peas (chana dal)
½ a large onion or 1 small onion, finely chopped
Handful of coriander leaves, finely chopped
Green chillies, finely chopped (optional)
2 tsp coriander powder
2 tsp mango powder
2 tsp curry powder
½ tsp paprika or 1 tsp chilli powder (opt.)
Salt to taste
Sunflower or olive oil

1. Soak the lentils for 3 to 4 hours in warm water or overnight in cold water.
2. Drain the water from the lentils and put them in a blender. Add 140ml of water or a little bit more and whizz it up to make a thick paste; the consistency should resemble that of cake batter.
3. Take the batter out in a bowl and add the onion, coriander leaves and all the spices and salt. Do not add green chillies or chilli powder if you don't want your bhajis to be spicy hot.
4. In a frying pan, add 6-8 tbsp of oil (or more) and heat well.
5. Lower the heat, and then carefully add a dollop of the lentil batter with a tablespoon into the hot oil.
6. Fry both sides evenly until it's golden brown in colour. Fry for approximately 8 mins on low heat. You can cut one in half to check the inside is cooked.
7. You can cook 5 to 6 bhajis in the pan at the same time.
8. Once they are cooked, take them out and place on kitchen towel to soak up the excess oil.
9. Serve with sweet chilli dip or mango chutney. These are great as a starter.

Note: When making the batter, add little water at a time in the blender so that it attains the right constituency. If the batter is too thin then you may add a few tablespoons of plain flour or gram flour to thicken it.

Cashew Chicken Curry

Serves 3-4

500g boneless chicken (preferably thigh fillets)
1 medium onion, finely chopped
3 cloves of garlic, finely chopped
1 inch sized piece of ginger, finely chopped
2 tbsp tomato puree
Coriander, finely chopped
150ml (approx.) of single cream
40-50g cashew nuts
½ tsp paprika or 1 tsp chilli powder
1 tsp turmeric powder
2 tsp coriander powder
1 tsp garam masala
2 cardamom pods
1 small piece of cinnamon stick
Salt to taste
Oil or butter

1. Cut the boneless chicken into small cubes, approximately 1 inch pieces.
2. Add 130ml of water (or a little more) to the cashew nuts and blend to a paste. Put aside.
3. Heat 2-3 tbsp of oil or 1-2 tbsp butter in a deep non-stick pan on a medium heat, and add the chopped onion, ginger and garlic. Sauté until browned.
4. Add 3 to 4 tbsp of water and then add all the spices, salt, and tomato purée. Cook for around 5 to 10 minutes, mixing well.
5. Add the chicken and stir well for 5 mins or more. Add approximately 250ml of water according to how much sauce you would prefer. Let it simmer for 15 minutes, half covered with the lid. Take out the cardamom pods and cinnamon stick and discard them if you wish.
6. Pour in the cream and cook for another 10 minutes.
7. Add the cashew paste and chopped coriander, stirring continuously.
8. Let it simmer for a further 10 minutes and then take off the heat. This is best served with basmati rice or chapatis, or naan or garlic bread.

Note: Do add sliced green chillies for a spicier taste.

Creamy Paneer

Serves 4

250g paneer
½ a large onion (preferably white), finely chopped
2 cloves of garlic, grated
1 inch sized ginger, grated
1 and ½ tbsp. tomato purée
50g of cashews
12-14 almonds
10g of raisins
150ml of single cream
2 cardamom pods
2 tsp coriander powder
½ tsp kasuri methi (dried fenugreek leaves)
½ tsp paprika or chilli powder (optional)
½ tsp garam masala powder
½ tsp turmeric
A pinch of nutmeg
A pinch of mace
Salt to taste
2 to 3 tbsp oil
1 tbsp butter
Pomegranate seeds (to garnish)

1. Soak the almonds in water for about 2 hours prior to cooking and peel them.
2. In a blender, add the cashews, almonds and raisins along with approximately 250ml of water and blend to a smooth paste.
3. Cut the paneer into small ½ inch size cubes. Heat the oil in a deep non-stick pan. When the oil is very hot, turn the heat down to low, and then carefully add the paneer cubes. Stand back as this can splutter quite a lot.
4. Cover immediately with a lid and let it cook for a couple of minutes. Once the spluttering dies down, half open the lid and turn the paneer cubes over to ensure even colouring.
5. Once they have turned light brown, transfer them into a bowl of hot water which will make them soft. Keep aside.
6. Now heat the butter in the same pan and add the chopped onion, ginger and garlic sautéing till light brown.
7. Next add the tomato purée, all the spices and salt, along with 2 to 3 tbsp of water. Mix well until it forms a smooth paste and let it cook for about 5 minutes, stirring in between.

8 Now add the paneer and about 250ml of water. Let it simmer for 15 minutes on low heat stirring once or twice in between.

9 Add the cream and let it simmer for a further 5 minutes stirring in between.

10 Finally, add the cashew paste and simmer for 10 minutes stirring frequently as the cashews have a tendency to burn easily.

11 Take off the heat and serve immediately. Pomegranate seeds can be used to garnish the dish.

Slow-cooked Lamb

Serves 3-4

500g diced lamb
½ a large onion or 1 whole small onion, finely chopped
4-5 cloves of garlic, finely grated
1.5 inch piece of ginger, finely grated
1 big ripe tomato, finely chopped or ½ tin chopped tomatoes
3 medium sized potatoes, peeled and cut in half
1 level tbsp of tomato puree (omit if using tinned tomatoes)
2 tsp turmeric powder
2 tsp coriander powder
1 tsp garam masala powder
½ tsp ground pepper (black or white)
½ tsp asafoetida powder (optional)
¼ tsp paprika or chilli powder
Fresh green chillies (optional)
1 tbsp kasuri methi or a handful of finely chopped fresh coriander
Salt to taste
150ml fresh single cream
Oil, ghee or butter

Whole Spices:
4 cardamom pods
1 inch cinnamon stick
2 cloves

1. Grind the whole spices in a blender with 50ml of water. Strain the mixture through a fine sieve and keep the flavoured water to one side. The residue spices may be discarded.
2. Marinate the lamb for an hour or so with 1 tbsp of oil and all of the powdered spices, except the asafoetida powder and salt.
3. Heat 2-3 tbsp of ghee, butter or oil in a deep pan. Fry the potatoes until they're golden on the outside. Remove from the pan to keep aside for later.
4. Now add the onions, garlic and ginger paste to the pan, and sautée until light brown.
5. Add the chopped tomatoes, tomato purée (omit if using tinned tomatoes), asafoetida powder, and 2 tbsp of water, and cook for about 5 minutes until everything is well combined.
6. Add the lamb to the pan and stir thoroughly for about 20 minutes. Add salt and the kasuri methi or coriander.
7. Pour in 250ml of water and stir well. Next add the spice-flavoured water along with the fried potatoes.

8 Now transfer the meat to a slow cooker and cook for 3-4 hours on a medium heat. If you don't have a slow cooker, cook on low heat on the hob for 2-3 hours, and cover with a lid. If you're cooking on the hob, you may need to add more water now and again to prevent it burning at the bottom. You may also use a pressure cooker to cook the meat, in which case you'll need to use about 400ml of water and cook it for about 45 minutes.

9 Halfway through the cooking time, add the cream along with the optional green chillies and give it a good stir. Let it cook for the remaining time.

10 Remove from heat and serve with basmati rice or chapatis.

Cauliflower, Lentils and Peas

Serves 4-6

1 medium or large cauliflower
4 small potatoes
Approximately 150g peas, frozen or fresh
2 inch piece of ginger, finely grated
2 tbsp tomato puree
1 medium tomato, finely chopped
1 tsp turmeric powder
2 tsp coriander powder
1 tsp cumin powder
1 tsp amchur (mango) powder (optional - if not available, use 1 tsp curry powder)
1 tsp garam masala powder
A handful of fresh coriander, finely chopped
Salt to taste
Oil or butter

1. Peel the potatoes and cut them in half. Cut the cauliflower into medium-sized florets. Keep to one side.
2. Heat 2-3 tbsp of oil or butter in a non-stick pan and add the potatoes. Lightly fry for 2 minutes, then add the cauliflower florets. Fry both for approximately 4-5 minutes until they are light brown in colour.
3. Now add the chopped tomato and the puree, stirring thoroughly.
4. Add all of the spices and the salt, along with the grated ginger. At this stage, add 3-4 tbsp of water so that the powdered spices don't burn. Cook for 5-7 minutes on a medium heat.
5. Add the chopped coriander leaves and pour in 400-500ml of water, according to your requirements, and half cover the pan with a lid. Simmer for 25 minutes or so on a low heat.
6. Take off the flame and serve with rice or chapatis.
7. Garnish with a few strips of coloured pepper.

Note: Those who like it spicy may add 2 tsp or more of mango or mixed vegetable pickle to the cauliflower. Stir it well for 2 to 3 minutes before taking it off the heat.

Chickpea Curry

Serves 6-8

4 tins of chickpeas, in water (approx. 900g)
1 large onion or 2 small onions, finely chopped
2 inch piece of ginger, crushed
6 cloves of garlic, crushed
½ tin of chopped tomatoes or 2 fresh tomatoes, finely chopped
1 level tbsp turmeric powder
1 tsp garam masala
2 tsp coriander powder
1 tsp paprika or 1 tsp chilli powder (optional)
1 tsp kasuri methi or a handful of finely chopped fresh coriander
2 sliced green chillies (optional)
2 tsp of chole masala (optional) or 2 tsp of mild curry powder
1 tbsp chaat masala or 1 tbsp mango powder
A pinch of asafoetida
Salt to taste
2-3 tbsp oil, ghee or butter

1. Drain the chickpeas and wash them thoroughly in a sieve or colander. Alternatively, soak raw chickpeas overnight and cook in a pressure cooker for half an hour, or a slow cooker for 3 hours with as much water as required and ¼ tsp salt.
2. Heat the oil, ghee or butter in a pan on a medium heat. Add the onions, ginger and garlic, and sauté until light brown, stirring frequently (for approximately 8-10 minutes).
3. Now add the chopped tomatoes, the spices and salt, along with 2 tbsp of water. Keep stirring until it forms a smooth mixture.
4. Add the chickpeas and around 600ml of water. Half cover the pan with a lid and let it simmer for 25 minutes on a low heat.
5. Finally add the chopped coriander and sliced green chillies if you prefer it hot. Take off the heat. This dish is delicious with puris, chapattis or buttered naan.

Note: For those who like it spicier, you may want to add a few drops of Tabasco sauce before serving.

Chickpea Curry

Serves 6-8

4 tins of chickpeas, in water (approx. 900g)
1 large onion or 2 small onions, finely chopped
2 inch piece of ginger, crushed
6 cloves of garlic, crushed
½ tin of chopped tomatoes or 2 fresh tomatoes, finely chopped
1 level tbsp turmeric powder
1 tsp garam masala
2 tsp coriander powder
1 tsp paprika or 1 tsp chilli powder (optional)
1 tsp kasuri methi or a handful of finely chopped fresh coriander
2 sliced green chillies (optional)
2 tsp of chole masala (optional) or 2 tsp of mild curry powder
1 tbsp chaat masala or 1 tbsp mango powder
A pinch of asafoetida
Salt to taste
2-3 tbsp oil, ghee or butter

1. Drain the chickpeas and wash them thoroughly in a sieve or colander. Alternatively, soak raw chickpeas overnight and cook in a pressure cooker for half an hour, or a slow cooker for 3 hours with as much water as required and ¼ tsp salt.
2. Heat the oil, ghee or butter in a pan on a medium heat. Add the onions, ginger and garlic, and sauté until light brown, stirring frequently (for approximately 8-10 minutes).
3. Now add the chopped tomatoes, the spices and salt, along with 2 tbsp of water. Keep stirring until it forms a smooth mixture.
4. Add the chickpeas and around 600ml of water. Half cover the pan with a lid and let it simmer for 25 minutes on a low heat.
5. Finally add the chopped coriander and sliced green chillies if you prefer it hot. Take off the heat. This dish is delicious with puris, chapattis or buttered naan.

Note: For those who like it spicier, you may want to add a few drops of Tabasco sauce before serving.

Puris

Makes 12-15 Puris

175g plain flour
175g wheat flour
Water to make a dough
A pinch of salt
600 ml of oil (only for deep-frying!)

1. Mix the two cups of flour with 1 tbsp of oil and a pinch of salt. Add a little water at a time to make a tight dough. If the dough is tight, the puris will puff up more.
2. Divide the dough into small, equal-sized balls (roughly 1.5 inches in diameter).
3. Put a couple of drops of oil on the surface on to which you're going to roll out the puris. Now take one ball at a time and roll it out into a circle of about 4 inches in diameter. Roll it out once with a bit of pressure, then lift the rolling pin and turn the dough round before rolling it out again. Rotating the dough after every stretch will stop it sticking to the surface. The puris must be really thin when stretched out.
4. Heat the oil in a small, deep pan until very hot.
5. Lower one puri into the hot oil and press it down slightly with a wooden spoon and then let go. Wait for the puri to puff up in the oil. Turn it over once and cook the other side for about 30 seconds (until golden brown in colour) before taking it out on some kitchen towel to soak up the excess oil.

   These are perfect served with chickpea curry, butter chicken, or slow cooked lamb curry.

Note: You may roll out all of the dough on the surface and use 3-4 inch diameter cookie cutters to cut out even shaped puris. The puris should be only a few millimetres thick.

It is better to use a deep pan to fry the puris in. You may want to put more than 600ml of oil so the puri puffs up well. When you drop each puri into the pan, the oil must be very hot. However, once the puri is in the pan, lower the heat so they don't burn. You will have to keep adjusting the heat accordingly.

Butter Chicken

Serves 3-4

500g boneless chicken, preferably thigh fillet
2 small onions or 1 big onion
1 medium tomato, finely chopped
1 tbsp tomato purée
6 cloves of garlic, grated
1 inch piece of ginger, grated
3 levelled tbsp of yogurt
1 tsp turmeric powder
2 tsp coriander powder
1 tsp cumin powder
½ tsp paprika or ½ tsp chilli powder
½ tsp garam masala powder
Handful of coriander leaves, chopped finely
1 tsp kasuri methi
3 tbsp ghee or butter
Salt to taste
A pinch of sugar (optional)
Green chillies (optional)

Whole Spices:
4 peppercorns
2 cardamoms
1 inch size cinnamon stick
2 cloves

1. Cut the chicken into pieces around 1 inch in size and keep to one side.
2. Grind the whole spices with 50ml of water in a blender. Strain the mixture with a sieve. Discard the residue and keep the flavoured water aside.
3. Heat the ghee or butter in a pan and add the chopped onions, garlic and ginger. Fry them on a low heat for 10 minutes or so, until they are light brown in colour.
4. Add the tomatoes to the pan. Mix together until well combined.
5. Add all the powdered spices and salt with about 2 tbsp of water and stir for 5-8 minutes.
6. Add the chicken to the pan and pour the yogurt in, stirring continuously.
7. Let it cook for about 10 minutes, before adding approximately 175ml of water, or more according to your preference.

8 Let it cook on low heat for 20 minutes. Half cover the pan with a lid. Stir once or twice in between.

9 Now add the fresh coriander, a sprinkle of sugar (if required) and the spice-flavoured water.

10 Cook for a further 5 minutes on low heat. Take off the heat and serve with mixed vegetable and prawn fried rice (see page 35), basmati rice, chappati, or naan bread.

Note: For one kilo of chicken, use three or four small onions. The spices may then all be doubled in quantity.

Red Lentils

Serves 4-6

200g red split lentils
Half an onion, chopped finely
2 cloves of garlic, grated
1 small tomato, chopped finely
Handful of coriander, chopped finely
Green chillies (optional)

1 tbsp butter or ghee
Approximately 500ml of water
¼ tsp turmeric powder
¼ tsp paprika or mild chilli powder
Salt to taste

1. Boil the lentils in about 500ml of water with the turmeric and salt, for approximately 20-30 minutes until they soften. Keep to one side.
2. Heat the butter in a deep pan and add the chopped onions and grated garlic. Fry until lightly browned.
3. Add the chopped tomato and other spices. Mix well.
4. Now pour in the boiled lentils and add the coriander. Simmer for about 5 minutes before taking off the heat. You may garnish with one or two slit green chillies if you like it hot. This dish is best served with hot basmati rice or chapatis.

Note: The lentils may become quite thick and so you may need to pour in some extra boiling water to achieve a thick soup-like consistency.

Stuffed Peppers with Keema

Serves 6

500g minced lamb
6 peppers (of different colours)
1 large onion, finely chopped
2 medium carrots, grated
4 cloves of garlic, grated
1 inch piece of ginger, grated
1 big tomato, finely chopped
Handful of fresh coriander, finely chopped
2 tbsp tomato purée
1 tbsp kasuri methi (dried fenugreek leaves)
½ a lime (optional)
1 tbsp coriander powder
1 tbsp cumin powder
1 tsp garam masala
1 tsp paprika or 1 tsp chilli powder (option)
½ tsp white or black ground pepper
A pinch of nutmeg powder
A pinch of mace powder
Oil or butter
Salt to taste

1. Cut off the tops of the peppers and scoop out the seeds. Keep the tops of the peppers to use as lids later. Sit the peppers on a lined baking tray.
2. In a deep non-stick pan, heat 2-3 tbsp of oil or butter and add the onions, garlic and ginger. Lightly fry for about 5 minutes until browned.
3. Add the chopped tomatoes and tomato purée, stirring well for about 5-7 minutes.
4. Next add the lamb, grated carrots, all the spices, salt and coriander. Cook for about 5-10 minutes on a medium heat, stirring well. Mix thoroughly until all the spices cover the meat. Add a few tbsp of water if necessary.
5. Half cover the pan with a lid and cook for about 20-25 minutes on a low heat, stirring once or twice in between. Now pre-heat the oven to 180°C.
6. At this stage, take the lid off and check if the meat stuffing is reasonably dry. If it's not, then increase the heat to dry off the excess liquid, as this will make it easier to stuff the peppers.
7. Take it off the flame, and let it cool for about 10 minutes. At this stage, you can squeeze the half lime into the stuffing if you wish.

8 Now stuff the peppers with the meat and loosely cover with the pepper tops.

9 Lightly drizzle the peppers with some olive oil before putting them in the oven.

10 Let them cook for about 30-45 minutes approximately at 180°C, or longer if necessary. Check once or twice in between to see the peppers don't burn.

11 Take the peppers out of the oven and serve with plain or garlic naan or garlic bread.

Note: You may add a few drops of Tabasco sauce or hot pepper sauce to the mince meat if you like it hot and spicy.

Paneer, Potatoes and Peas

Serves 3-4

250g paneer
2 medium potatoes
100g fresh or frozen peas
1 big fresh tomato
1 tbsp tomato puree
2 inch sized piece of ginger, grated
½ a big onion or 1 small onion, finely chopped
½ tsp turmeric powder
2 tsp coriander powder
½ tsp garam masala
½ tsp paprika or 1 tsp chilli powder
1 tsp cumin powder
2 whole cardamom pods
1 inch stick of cinnamon
1 tsp of kasuri methi (optional)
Salt to taste
Oil, ghee or butter

1. Peel the potatoes and boil them. Let them cool, then cut them into small pieces (approximately ½ inch each).
2. Cut the paneer into roughly 1 inch-sized cubes.
3. Heat 2 to 3 tbsp of the oil, ghee or butter in a deep non-stick pan until very hot. Now lower the heat and carefully add the paneer, and fry for about 5 minutes until light brown. You may need to keep the pan covered as paneer has a tendency to splutter quite a lot.
4. Take the lightly fried paneer and immerse in a bowl of warm water. This helps to soften the paneer.
5. Now in the same pan, lightly fry the potatoes and keep aside.
6. Add more oil, ghee or butter to the same pan again, and then add the chopped onions, ginger, cinnamon and cardamom. Fry on a low heat till light brown, stirring occasionally.
7. Next add the chopped tomatoes, tomato puree, salt, and all the spices along with 2 to 3 tbsp of water.

8 Finally add the paneer, potatoes and peas to the pan, and pour in about 400ml of water.

9 Let it simmer for 15 minutes. Keep the pan half covered during cooking.

10 Take it off the heat and serve with basmati rice, puris or chapatis.

Note: If you wish, you may discard the cinnamon stick and cardamon pods before serving.

Aubergines with Sun-dried Tomatoes

Serves 4-5

2 medium sized aubergines
130g drained sundried tomatoes
2 packs of baby button mushrooms*
1 large onion, finely chopped
1 pepper, finely chopped
4 cloves of garlic, crushed
1 inch size ginger, finely grated
1 tbsp tomato purée
½ tsp turmeric powder
½ tsp paprika or 1 tsp chilli powder (optional)
1 tsp ground coriander powder
1 tsp mild curry powder (optional)
½ tsp garam masala powder
Salt to taste
Butter or oil
A few drops of mild Tabasco (optional)
Handful of fresh coriander, finely chopped
Green chillies (optional)

**or 8-10 large mushrooms, quartered*

1. Chop the aubergines into small cubes (approximately 1 inch). Take off the mushroom stalks if you wish. Wash the mushrooms thoroughly and keep aside.
2. Heat 2 to 3 tbsp of butter or oil in a deep non-stick pan and add the mushrooms. Sauté the mushrooms until light brown, then remove from the pan and keep aside.
3. Pour a little more oil in the same pan if necessary, and add the onions, pepper, ginger and garlic, and gently fry until light brown.
4. Now add all of the spices, salt, sun-dried tomatoes and tomato purée, along with 2-3 tbsp of water, and stir together until well combined for approximately 5 minutes or so.
5. Add the aubergines and mushrooms with 140ml water. Half cover the pan with a lid and let it simmer for about 20-25 minutes, stirring once or twice whilst cooking.
6. Finish with a sprinkling of coriander leaves and, if you like it hot and spicy, a few drops of Tabasco or green chillies. Let it cook for a further 5 minutes.
7. Take off the heat and serve with steamed basmati rice, chapatis, or even garlic bread.

Mixed Vegetable and Prawn Fried Rice

Serves 3-4

250g rice
250g small cooked or raw prawns
85g long green beans, finely chopped
¼ of a cauliflower, finely chopped
2 medium carrots, finely chopped
1 large white onion, finely chopped
Handful of fresh or frozen peas
50g cashew nuts (optional)
40g raisins (optional)
¼ tsp turmeric or a pinch of saffron
¼ tsp ginger powder
2 bay leaves
4 cardamom pods
1 star anise
1 inch size cinnamon stick
Salt to taste
A pinch of sugar (optional)
Ghee, butter or oil

1. If you're using saffron, soak it in about 125ml of hot water and keep aside for two hours prior to cooking.
2. Boil the rice in plenty of water with the star anise and the cardamom, and then strain and keep aside. You may run cold water through it in a colander. It is important that the rice is not overcooked. Each grain should be separate and should not stick together.
3. Sprinkle some turmeric on the prawns and gently fry them in a pan with 1 to 2 tsbp of oil for a couple of minutes and keep to one side. If you wish to use cashew nuts instead of prawns, fry the cashews in a tbsp of butter and keep to one side.
4. Heat 2-3 tbsp of the ghee, butter or oil in a deep non-stick pan and add the bay leaves and cinnamon stick.
5. Next add the onions and ginger powder and sauté for a few minutes on low heat.
6. Add the rest of the chopped vegetables along with the salt. If you are using saffron, strain the coloured water into the pan at this stage. If you're using turmeric instead, add the turmeric powder along with 125ml of water. Cover the pan completely and cook for 10 minutes on low heat. Now check to see if the vegetables are cooked.
7. Finally, add the rice and the prawns or cashew nuts to the pan. You may add raisins too if you wish. Mix well and take off the heat. This is excellent served with butter chicken (see page 24) or slow cooked lamb (see page 16).

Pineapple Chutney

Serves 8-10

800g pineapple chunks (peeled)
50g raisins
100g granulated sugar
½ inch size ginger, crushed
A pinch of turmeric
A few drops of lemon juice
10-12 whole mustard seeds
½ a dried red chilli (optional)
A pinch of salt
350ml water
Oil

1. Cut the pineapple chunks into small pieces.
2. Heat 2 tbsp of oil in a deep non-stick pan. Add the whole mustard seeds and the red chilli. Be careful as this may splutter.
3. Now add all the pineapple chunks, a pinch of turmeric, a pinch of salt and squeeze in a few pinches of the crushed ginger. Stir well and then add all the water and the raisins. Half cover the pan with a lid and let it simmer for 20 minutes.
4. Now add the sugar and let it cook for another 5 minutes, stirring well.
5. Take it off the heat and add a couple of drops of lemon juice if you prefer.
6. Let it cool and then put the chutney in the refrigerator. Serve chilled. This is a great accompaniment with any kind of vegetable or meat curries.

Note: Dried whole red chillies are very hot, so use it only if you like it spicy!

Aloo Parathas

Serves 6

6 medium potatoes
½ a big onion, finely chopped
25g mild cheddar cheese, finely grated
1 tsp coriander powder
½ tsp cumin powder
½ tsp garam masala
1 tsp dry mango powder or curry powder (optional)
½ tsp paprika
Handful of fresh coriander leaves, finely chopped
Salt to taste
Butter or oil
350g wheat flour
Water to make dough

1 Boil the potatoes and mash them till smooth. Add the fresh coriander, all the powdered spices, salt and the grated cheese to the mash. Mix until all the ingredients are well combined and put to one side.

2 In a large bowl, make a soft dough with the flour and water, kneading well. Divide the dough equally into balls of approximately 2 inches in diameter.

3 Take one dough ball at a time and spread it out on your palm to make a pocket. Fill it with about 2 tbsp of the potato stuffing and fold and seal the edges with your fingers.

4 Sprinkle some flour on the surface on which you will roll out the parathas. Now gently pat it flat, and using a rolling pin, roll it out into a flat circular shape (they should resemble chapattis at this stage). Be very gentle when rolling so that the stuffing does not pop out.

5 Heat a flat non-stick pan without any oil and toss the paratha on it a couple times until it is lightly browned on both sides.

6 Now spread about ½ tbsp of butter or oil on both sides of the paratha and toss again for a couple of times until the paratha is cooked. It should be a golden brown in colour when you take it off the heat.

7 Take it out of the pan and immediately wrap it in aluminium foil to keep it warm and soft. These can be served with many accompaniments such as mango chutney, mango pickles, white yoghurt or hummus.

Note *Each paratha has to be cooked well for approximately 5-8 mins to attain the right taste.*

Cucumber Raita

Serves 5-6

500g natural yoghurt
¼ of a cucumber
½ a tomato, seeds removed
¼ of a small onion, finely chopped
½ tsp cumin powder
A pinch of paprika
A pinch of black rock salt*
Finely chopped coriander for garnishing

**also known as 'Kala Namak'. If this isn't available, you can just use ordinary salt.*

1. Peel the cucumber and finely chop it into little cubes, or into long matchstick shaped pieces, whichever you prefer.
2. Chop the onion, tomato (deseeded) and coriander finely, and keep aside.
3. Put the yoghurt in a bowl with the spices and salt, and beat with a fork until it becomes smooth. If you want a slightly thinner Raita, you can add approximately 80ml of water at this stage and beat until smooth.
4. Now add the cucumber, onion and tomato and mix them in well.
5. Finally, garnish with a sprinkling of the fresh coriander. This is a perfect accompaniment to almost any kind of curry!

Note: *For the perfect Raita, chop the vegetables as finely as possible. The amount of water can be adjusted according to how thick or thin you want the Raita to be.*

Long Green Beans with Coconut

Serves 3-4

450g of long green beans, finely chopped
100g desiccated coconut or 100g fresh coconut, grated
½ tsp whole mustard seeds
6-8 dried curry leaves
½ dried red chilli (optional)
1 inch-size piece of ginger, finely grated
¼ tsp turmeric powder
¼ tsp paprika or chilli powder
A pinch of asafoetida powder
Salt to taste
Oil

1. Heat 2-3 tbsp of oil in a deep non-stick pan. Add the curry leaves, the mustard seeds, ginger, and the dried red chilli.
2. Now add the beans and stir well for 5 minutes.
3. Next add the salt, turmeric and asafoetida powder, and pour in approximately 150ml of water and cover the pan completely with a lid.
4. Let it simmer for 20 minutes on a low heat, stirring once or twice in between.
5. Finally add the grated coconut and stir well for about 5 minutes. If there is still some water in the pan, increase the heat and cook until the water has evaporated completely. Stir often as coconut tends to burn easily.
6. Remove from heat and serve with basmati rice.

Okra with Cherry Tomatoes and Onions

Serves 4-5

500g okra
1 large onion, finely chopped
8-10 cherry tomatoes, cut in half (or 1 large tomato, finely chopped)
1 tbsp tomato puree
½ tsp turmeric powder
½ tsp paprika or 1 tsp chilli powder (optional)
2 tsp coriander powder
1 tsp chaat masala powder (optional)
½ tsp garam masala
Salt to taste
2-3 tbsp of sunflower or olive oil

1. Wash the okra and dry them thoroughly with kitchen towel. This ensures that the okra doesn't become slimy when it is being cooked.
2. Top and tail the okra, then chop each one into 2 or 3 pieces according to their size.
3. Now heat the oil in a pan and add the chopped onions. Sauté until they turn light brown in colour.
4. Next add the cherry tomatoes, all the spices and salt, mixing well.
5. Now stir in the okra and let it simmer on low heat for approximately 25 to 30 minutes, half covering the pan with a lid. Stir gently once or twice in between, being careful not to stir too often as this can lead to the okra becoming sticky.
6. Take off the heat and serve with lentils and rice.

Spinach Paneer Curry

Serves 4

250g paneer
120g baby spinach
½ large onion, finely chopped
4 cloves of garlic, finely chopped
Thumb-sized piece of ginger, grated
2 small tomatoes
50ml of single cream
Green chillies (optional)
1 tbsp of kasuri methi leaves (optional)
½ tsp chaat masala
½ tsp cumin powder
¼ tsp turmeric powder
½ tsp coriander powder
½ tsp red chilli powder
½ tsp garam masala
Salt to taste
Oil (to fry paneer)
Ghee or butter

1. Cut the paneer into small half-inch cubes. Heat about 2 tbsp of oil in a pan and lightly fry the paneer cubes until they turn light brown in colour. Do this on low heat for about 5 minutes and cover the pan with a lid as the paneer can splutter.
2. Remove from the pan and transfer to a bowl of very hot water. Soaking the paneer cubes in hot water makes them softer.
3. Add the ghee or butter to the pan and sauté the finely chopped ginger and garlic in it. Add the onions and cook for a further 5 minutes on low heat until the onion becomes translucent. Now turn the heat up to medium and fry for a further 3-4 minutes until the onions become light brown in colour.
4. Chop the tomatoes in half and put them in an electric food chopper or a blender to grind to a chunky purée.
5. Add the tomatoes to the pan and cook with the onions. At this stage add the salt, and all the spices EXCEPT the garam masala, along with 2 tbsp of water. Cook for a further 5 minutes, stirring well.
6. Meanwhile, put all of the spinach in a blender and pour 200ml of boiling water over the top. Leave to stand for a couple of minutes until the leaves wilt slightly. Now blend it into a smooth purée.

7 Add the spinach purée to the pan and stir well. Drain the paneer and add to the pan, stirring gently so as to not break the soft paneer cubes. You may add chopped green chillies at this stage if you wish. Simmer for 10 minutes on a low heat.

8 Pour in the single cream and then add the garam masala. Finally, add the kasuri methi leaves (this can be substituted with fresh coriander leaves) and give it a good stir. Let it simmer for a couple of minutes and then take it off the heat. This is a very nutritious curry and can be served with rice or chapattis.

Salmon in a Mustard Sauce

Serves 2

2 fillets of salmon (approx. 250g total), skinless
1 ripe medium-sized tomato, finely chopped
4-6 fresh or dried curry leaves
2-3 tbsp of natural yogurt
Whole or slit green chillies (optional)
1 tsp turmeric powder
½ tsp paprika or 1 tsp chilli powder
1 tsp original English mustard paste
Salt to taste
Sunflower or olive oil

1. Cut the salmon into roughly 3x1 inch pieces. Sprinkle a little salt and a ¼ tsp of the turmeric on the fish.
2. Heat 2 to 3 tbsp of oil in a deep non-stick pan until very hot. Lower the heat and carefully add the fish, preferably 2 pieces at a time. Lightly fry the fish pieces on both sides until they are golden in colour. Take them out of the pan and put to one side.
3. Now in the same pan (adding more oil if necessary) add the curry leaves and the chopped tomatoes, along with the paprika, the rest of the turmeric and salt. Add 2 tbsp of water and stir well for 3 minutes or so.
4. Next, add the yogurt and mix until well combined.
5. Return the salmon to the pan, and stir gently, being careful not to break the pieces of fish.
6. Now pour in about 175ml of water and simmer for approximately 10 minutes.
7. Finally, add the English mustard and green chillies (optional) and mix well.
8. Remove from the heat and serve hot with rice or couscous.

Note: *If you don't want to use English mustard, you can make a mustard paste at home with 1 heaped tbsp of whole black mustard seeds. Just blend the mustard seeds and 100ml of water in a blender to make a smooth paste. This also works well with prawns and hilsa, a fish commonly found in India.*

I love Indian food but I have often been disappointed in the dishes I have ordered in restaurants over the years. I was therefore very excited when I discovered that, through using Aloka's recipes, I could make authentic Indian food in my own home that tastes delicious. Aloka's recipes are very easy to follow, even for a complete novice like me, and my family's favourite recipe is Creamy Paneer. I have been able to get all the ingredients in my local supermarket which is essential for me as a busy mum. The recipes have the added bonus of being healthy, and many of them are vegetarian too. I am grateful to Aloka for demystifying the spices and techniques used in Indian cooking. Her recipes are highly recommended.

Berit Lindholm (Airline pilot)

Aloka's Kitchen really opened my eyes to authentic Indian cooking. It felt like being let into a very special secret. Aloka puts so much care in to every stage of the process: selecting ingredients, coming up with recipes, and making things very easy to follow. Her passion and expertise shines through. The whole experience was professional – but also great fun!"

Andrew Wilson (Journalist and Editor)

It's surprising how a fast food loving person like me got fond of home cooked food. There are many dishes that I never used to like before marriage which I now relish when cooked by Aloka. I am fortunate to taste her delicious, appetising food every day and I am pleasantly surprised with the new dishes she creates. Aloka has the knack of cooking which comes from within and I am sure you will all enjoy her special recipes."

Sandeep Ray (Global Director Sales, Datamine)

WESTERN MANAGER

The photographs of Lance Ibbotson MBE
BR Western Region 1959-63
Selected and captioned by Will Adams

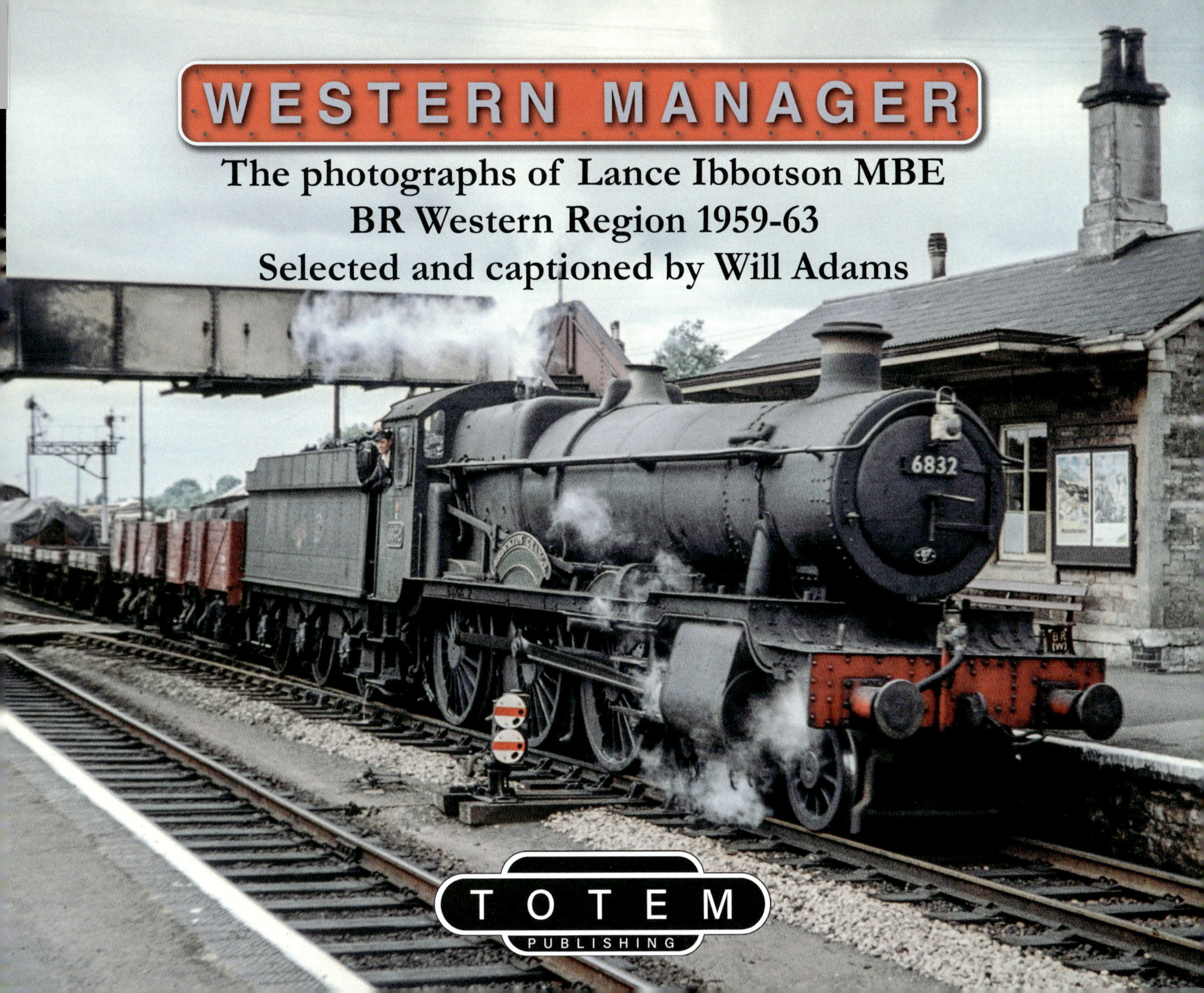

TOTEM
PUBLISHING

This book is dedicated to Peter Upton (1926 - 2002)

ISBN 978-1-917776-01-1

First published in 2025 by Transport Treasury Publishing Limited, 16 Highworth Close, High Wycombe HP13 7PJ

Totem Publishing is an imprint of Transport Treasury Publishing.

www.ttpublishing.co.uk

Printed in Tarxien, Malta By Gutenberg Printing Ltd.

'Western Manager' is one of a series of books on specialist transport subjects produced in strictly limited numbers under the Totem Publishing imprint using material only available to The Transport Treasury.

Front cover: Photographed on 26 March 1962, the day of Lance's visit to Plymouth, is 'Western' diesel-hydraulic No D1001 'Western Pathfinder', built at Swindon only a month or so earlier, having been released into traffic on 12 February 1962. As seen here, the locomotive was originally outshopped in maroon without yellow warning panels, only the buffer beam being so painted. On release 'Pathfinder' was used for trials against Brush's Class 47 prototype No D0280 'Falcon'. No D1001 was initially allocated to Plymouth's Laira depot, and was a frequent resident despite transfers to Old Oak Common and Swansea. Withdrawal came in October 1976 following damage received in a collision with a BR van, and it was cut up at its birthplace, Swindon, the following year.

Frontispiece: Most of Lance Ibbotson's pictures in this selection were taken during official visits to locations, giving us behind-the-scenes views of developments on the Western Region between 1959 and 1963. Here, though, is a straightforward shot of what was then a common sight on the Western, ex-GWR 'Grange' Class 4-6-0 No 6832 'Brockton Grange', heading an up mixed freight towards Chepstow and Gloucester through Portskewett station, north-east of Severn Tunnel Junction, in June 1961. A Llanelly-based locomotive at this time, it had another 2½ years of service left before withdrawal in January 1964; by November of that year Portskewett station had gone too.

Rear cover: Seen from Intercity House on 26 March 1962, this is the view across the west end of Plymouth station, with new buildings in the foreground and the new panel signal box on the left, next to the Saltash Road underbridge. On the far side of the station is the former Royal Mail sorting office (hence its direct access to the station above street level); this building is now incorporated into the University of Plymouth's Emdeck Building. In the station is an unidentified member of the North British-built D6xx 'Warship' Class, coupled to a BR-built D8xx example. Yet for all the newness, there's a steam-hauled passenger train in the down platform, its presence given away by the wisp of steam above the platform canopy; it appears to have smoke deflectors, so is perhaps a 'Britannia' 'Pacific'.

Contents and Introduction

Many years ago, when working as commissioning editor for a railway book publishing company, I was offered a biography of career railwayman Lance Ibbotson, written by Peter Upton. In the event we were unable to publish the book, but Mr Upton gave me a collection of colour transparencies taken by Mr Ibbotson during the course of his working life, most dating from the years 1959 to 1963 (together with some from 1967-68), when he was rising through the ranks of British Railways Western Region; he became General Manager in 1966, before moving to the same position on the Southern Region two years later. The pictures lay largely unused until, thanks to the encouragement of Kevin Robertson and Robin Fell of Transport Treasury Publishing, it was decided to compile a book featuring the best of these unique, often behind-the-scenes, views. The following details of Mr Ibbotson's life and career are drawn from Peter Upton's book, *On The Up Line*, which he published privately in 1992. It is often available second-hand, and is highly recommended as a detailed record of the complexities of railway operation and organisation over many decades, and one man's varied career within it. What follows is by necessity a very brief digest.

Lancelot William Cripps Ibbotson was born in Streatham, south London, on 10 February 1909. His grandfather had been a Master Cutler in the mid-19th century, Chairman of Ibbotson Brothers of Sheffield, while his grandfather was a Sheffield solicitor. His father was a GP, and had suffered greatly as a Ship's Doctor during the Great War. Following his separation from his wife Dora, she moved Lance and his siblings to Hampstead, to be nearer her work as a masseuse at Hampstead General Hospital.

Lance attended kindergarten in Highgate, while his older brother Cedric was at Highgate School, where he was a contemporary of John Betjeman. Lance followed him briefly, then at the age of nine went with him to board at Brighton College Preparatory School. Here his previous willful temperament was tamed, and he became a gifted Classics scholar. He was accomplished enough to be granted a scholarship to Radley College in Oxfordshire in 1922. His housemaster considered that he ought to be able to qualify for an Oxford Scholarship, but when interviewed at the age of 17 he was told that he was too immature – he would be reconsidered the following year. In the event he left Radley to look for a job.

Meanwhile his mother and grandparents had moved to Ealing, near the GWR main line. Lance made a model railway at the bottom of the garden, assisted by his grandfather. His father, although absent, had paid his fees at Radley, and also paid the rent on the Ealing house. He asked Lance what he intended to do with his life; his son had no idea, but the first thing that came into his head was a life on the railway. His father said, 'Oh yes, I operated on the daughter of one of the directors of the London North Eastern. I will see what I can do.'

In due course Lance received a letter from the Chief General Manager at King's Cross, inviting him to become a Traffic Apprentice, and after a brief interview he was appointed. Books arrived for him to study, dealing with organisation and operations, how to book tickets, how to book a horse, how to transport cows, and innumerable other instructions. The LNER took its Traffic Apprenticeship scheme very seriously, as an avenue for advancement for the promising leaders of the future. Apprentices were given three years of training, being sent to a variety of jobs in different places to gain the necessary experience.

Lance's initial posting was to Cullingworth, a small station between Bradford and Keighley, commencing on 1 April 1927. He was initially put on the 9.00am to 5.00pm shift as a trainee booking clerk, but after only three weeks training the position was made permanent, and he started work in that capacity on Easter Monday 1927 at a wage of £2 a week. He also handled parcels traffic going by passenger train. At this time he had lodgings in Shipley, his meagre income supplemented by an allowance of £100 a year from his father. During his apprenticeship his pay was increased by £10 a year. Anxious to progress, Lance wrote to the Assistant General Manager, and was given a minor move to the nearby station at Denholme, where the clerk also handled goods traffic. From there he moved to Shipley, where there was a large goods station.

While at Cullingworth a friend of his sister helped him to find lodgings, and he became a friend of the family. The friend was Joan Jeffcott; she was three years older than Lance, and a mutual attraction soon arose.

Lance next moved to Queen's Walk, Nottingham, the goods station of the former Great Central Railway. This was Lance's first experience of a large and busy station and a very challenging job for a learner. Goods outwards were largely consignments from Boots, Raleigh Cycles and Players Cigarettes.

Following that was the District Office in Nottingham, which controlled the commercial work of the city's stations and goods depots. Lance was also sent to Grimsby for a month, then the largest fish dock in the country, and thence to Immingham.

The next step in his apprenticeship took Lance to the large marshalling yard at Doncaster, which stretched for about 3 miles end to end and was in a state of permanent congestion. By this time he and Joan had fallen in love, and he proposed to her in a train at King's Cross. They agreed to marry as soon as they could afford to; Lance was still poorly paid.

The District Manager at Manchester, a Mr Pruce, took charge of Lance, who began to accompany him on his visits round the old Great Central District, including walking the 7 miles up the railway from Glossop to Woodhead, as well as visiting Annesley, the northern end of the GCR's 'London Extension'. Reports were filed on the overcrowding of lines and yards, but nothing was ever done, which Lance saw as a valuable lesson. He could see that the railway was run more by inspiration and good fellowship than by anything else.

His next move was to Scotland, where he reported to the Superintendent at Edinburgh and worked at Portobello marshalling yard. Here he witnessed for the first time an atmosphere of cooperation and pride that seemed lacking in England. His next assignment was to the marshalling yard at Cadder in Glasgow.

Lance (foreground) and Joan (standing, right), possibly on holiday with friends – date, location and occasion unknown.

He was again pleasantly surprised to see Scottish efficiency and punctuality, in particular the precision of the scheduling of trains moving south over the bottleneck of the Forth Bridge, not only on time and also in the correct order!

In a foreshadowing of the Beeching years, in 1929 he was asked to report on the usage and profitability of the many branch lines around Edinburgh, only to find them hopelessly inefficient and unprofitable. Meanwhile, at York the Operating Superintendent, Charles Jenkin-Jones, an Oxford Classical Scholar, was aware of the amount of time wasted by freight train crews, and in 1930 he assembled six keen young Traffic Apprentices to put together some kind of scheme to deal with this. Lance was one of them, and they worked together on the project for the next three years; he later regarded this as one of the most important things he was called upon to do on the railway. Another of the team was Freddie Margetts, who became a British Rail Board member many years later.

As a result of their detailed studies they became more knowledgeable about the working of the railway than perhaps anyone else at the time. They studied in particular the traditional 'pick-up' goods that travelled a line calling at all the intermediate stations to pick up and drop off wagons. They devised a bonus scheme that accelerated the job, and trains that had taken nine or ten hours to complete the job now did it in five. Jenkin-Jones was delighted with the result, and the scheme was expanded.

In October 1931 Joan and Lance married at York Registry Office. After a honeymoon in the West Country, they set up home in York.

Lance's team next turned their attention to inter-yard 'trip' goods working in the Newport and Middlesbrough area, and again the results of their bonus scheme in terms of economy and efficiency were remarkable. His apprenticeship completed, he began his railway career proper, and was appointed Assistant Yardmaster at West Hartlepool at the age of just 24. Here again his organisational abilities resulted in positive changes, despite the attitude of 'we've always done it this way'.

His next move was to the District Office at Darlington in 1935; as Head of the Passenger Train Section, he dealt with timetable and rolling stock issues in an area covering 120 stations. The Ibbotsons now had a larger house with gardens – they also had two children, Jonathan and Rhona, and could afford a maid.

Lance was next promoted as Head of the Freight Train Section, in control of the District Control Office at Darlington – a very busy and interesting job. In 1937 he returned to York to form part of a three-man squad to conduct an inquiry into freight operations over the whole North Eastern area – another interesting and exciting task that occupied two years, and involved extensive travel throughout the district. The team were in Berwick on the day that war was declared in 1939. A secondary job for Lance was the organisation and provision of camping coaches, including their contents!

On the outbreak of war Lance became Chief Clerk to the District Superintendent at Newcastle, looking after train operations; he also organised a scheme to get evacuated children away from the city. During the blackout working conditions were hard, but morale was high. He was later transferred back to York, where one of his tasks was to coordinate plans between the railway and the Army to cope with the threat of a German invasion; this involved immobilisation of locomotives and communications in the Hull area, a likely invasion point. Meanwhile in York he had to oversee the movement of heavy wartime traffic through the busy York hub; on one occasion there were 22 trains between Thirsk and York, all waiting to get into the city.

As the war drew to a close Lance was appointed District Superintendent at Sunderland, but before he could take up this post he was offered the more important job as Acting District Superintendent at Darlington, moving there in 1945. This was, of course, an area with which he was already familiar. He regularly visited all the stations, signal boxes and yards to get to know the staff and gauge the 'feel' of the railway. He considered this one of the most constructive periods of his career, and learned the importance of individual man management, getting to know as many staff members as possible, and how vital this was for the successful working of the railway. It would be a great help to him in his future career.

It was while Lance was at Darlington that the railways were nationalised, taking effect from 1 January 1948. Yet seemingly the day-to-day operations of the railway for the ordinary railwayman did not change a great deal.

That year Lance was awarded the CBE (MBE in 1971), which came as a pleasant surprise; he thought it was perhaps because he had overseen the successful transition from the old order to nationalisation in his district.

By 1950, now aged 41, Lance had made quite a name for himself during his time with the LNER, and he was suddenly offered the chance to move to the Western Region of BR, as Trains Assistant to the Operating Superintendent, Gilbert Matthews. It was unusual for the former GWR to appoint someone from outside 'God's

Possibly as a result of his investigations into the feasibility of electrifying the Western Region, Lance visited Wilmslow, East Didsbury and Sandbach in the spring of 1959. The route from Crewe to Manchester Piccadilly, including the Styal line, was the first section of the West Coast Main Line to be electrified, coming into operation in that year. This is the view looking north towards Sandbach station, at Rookery Bridge signal box (off the picture to the right). This was one of the boxes that closed as a result of the change to colour-light signalling, although it can be seen that semaphore signalling is still in use here, including some fine examples of LNWR ground signals. On the right is the Ettiley Heath salt works of Palmer Mann & Co, with its private siding; the company manufactured 'Sifta' table salt from 1919 until 1971.

Wonderful Railway'! Nonetheless, he was given the job, and he and his family moved south to West Drayton.

Although aware of the fact that he was a 'foreigner', Lance was impressed by the management structure. He soon became heavily involved with freight operations, his speciality, which had been somewhat neglected during the war. Lance brought his well-honed organisational abilities to bear on the planning and structuring of freight movements; by means of careful questioning and the establishment of inquiries he dealt with longstanding practices that needed revision, despite some opposition.

On the passenger side, Lance instituted a system of 'clock-face' train departures from Paddington, with Birmingham trains departing at 10 minutes past the hour, Worcester at 15 minutes past, and so on. Old hands regretted the loss of traditional departure times, but the system lasted successfully for many years. He also investigated the haphazardness and duplication of services in the Welsh valleys, and the running of holiday trains, especially to the West Country. In effect, the latter involved booking every passenger so that trains

Top: To control the new signalling a state-of-the-art signal box and control centre were built near the end of the Styal Line down platform at Wilmslow, serving almost the whole route from Crewe to Manchester via both routes. It was a non-standard BR structure, designed by William Headley (the architect employed by the LMR to design stations at East Didsbury, Manchester Piccadilly and Oxford Road, as well as Coventry, among others). The signal box, at the far end of this structure, contained a Westinghouse One Control Switch panel and opened on 26 June 1959. This and the other new power box at Sandbach controlled 27 miles between Crewe, Cheadle Hulme and Gatley, replacing 14 mechanical boxes. Wilmslow power box closed at the end of 2005 and was demolished when signalling controlled by Manchester South Signalling Control Centre was commissioned the following year.

Bottom: A rail-mounted auger for drilling the holes for the masts that supported the overhead line equipment.

no longer ran in duplicate or even triplicate, which led to grumbles but reduced delays considerably. One of Lance's colleagues, John Palette, felt that, after a little time, he had established himself as the architect of sensible change on the Western Region, reforming a system that, in John's words, had 'lasted since Adam was a lad'.

In the 1950s Lance was instructed to report on the feasibility of electrifying the WR; it had already been decided to replace steam with diesel and electric. After considering all the factors over a period of six months, the final recommendation was to go for diesel operation throughout. The BR Board ruled that the London Midland Region from London to Manchester would be electrified instead, and that the WR would elect to develop diesel-hydraulic locomotives rather than diesel-electric, as adopted elsewhere, which in the event turned out to be a poor choice.

Watching over railway operations became Lance's daily routine, a largely repetitive round of morning telephone conferences with all the regional operating staff to grapple with current problems, to resolve them and keep traffic on the move. It was a pressurised job. The routine was broken by a sudden and unexpected three-week visit to Russia, as the operating representative of a group of six other senior men; the Russians had toured BR the year before.

By the early 1960s Lance was somewhat frustrated at the lack of promotion opportunities, but was suddenly offered the job as Works Assistant, for New Projects, to the General Manager. Lance accepted gladly – the job would entail making decisions on the priority for future capital works. One of the main projects was the modernising of freight yards, including a new one at Margam, as we shall see later. Promoting another yard to be built at Gloucester, Lance had to appear before a House of Lords committee. He was able to deal with their searching questions with ease, but in the event the yard was never built. Nonetheless Lance enjoyed the experience, which was novel and stimulating.

In 1960 the family moved to a new post-war house in Porchester Gardens, within walking distance of Paddington.

Lance's next promotion was as Assistant General Manager (Traffic), shortly before Stanley Raymond became General Manager in January 1962. Stanley was dubbed 'the Whirlwind', and his attitude was very much akin to Lance's. He got round the whole Region in 72 hours and had an action plan ready in about seven days; his rapidity left even Lance gasping! Like Lance, he did not subscribe to the 'this is the way we have always done it' attitude. Stanley was well ahead of Dr Richard Beeching, whose infamous 'Reshaping' report was not published until 1963.

Beeching also requested a reorganisation of regional boundaries to provide a more efficient and economical service. The WR was to give up territory, and Lance was deputed to the task of defining the new boundaries. He considered that the WR's London-Birmingham Snow Hill services, duplicating those on the soon-to-be-electrified LMR, should be abandoned, that the Central Wales line should be passed to the Midland, and the summer-only Vale of Rheidol narrow-gauge line should be got rid of! He toured the affected areas with the LMR General Manager Bill Johnson, a good exercise in public relations. Western men were disappointed but largely accepted the situation. Lance was recognised as a person who made up his mind and knew what he wanted; he was also adept at trusting subordinates, allowing them to get on with their jobs and take personal responsibility.

In 1963 he was offered the job of Chief Operating Officer on the British Railways Board at Marylebone, which would be a change from his regional work. His immediate superior was Freddie Margetts, with whom he had worked at York in the 1930s. It was a rather contradictory post, as he was expected to ensure that operational work was efficiently conducted by the Regions, but prevented from overruling them if they thought otherwise. He did this difficult and demanding job for a year.

Like Lance, Dr Beeching was a man who quickly analysed problems and came up with workable solutions. Lance held him in high regard, and considered him the best of the BRB Chairmen he knew. He was sorry that he decided to leave in 1965 before his reforms were completed, due partly to the new Labour Government not supporting his policies. Beeching told Lance, 'I have really had enough; when your photo appears in the daily newspaper on about four days out of six, you feel the pressure quite intolerable. I shall be glad to leave.' He was succeeded by Stanley Raymond, who invited Lance to become WR General Manager; Lance enthusiastically accepted, and rejoined the Region in 1966.

Lance was, of course, no stranger to the WR, and followed some very popular and good General Managers – Keith Grand, Stanley Raymond and Gerard Fiennes. Despite having opposed some sensible reforms, the Region enjoyed a generally high standard of performance. Lance was keen to use his new position of authority to enhance the stature of the railway, and improve its commercial image. He held regular meetings with local MPs and the heads of local businesses, as well as senior staff members.

In 1965 Lance visited Canada and the USA to look at their modern methods for handling and transporting coal. However, the coal industry in the UK was in decline, and following a visit by Lance and Beeching to South Wales, Lance had to agree with the latter the collieries were doing better out of the railways than the railways were doing out of the collieries. Under Beeching the number of coal distribution depots was reduced and large new ones established, reducing the amount of individual wagon shunting required. Other previously important traffic – milk, oil and steel – was also declining, often as a result of increasing road transport.

Problems also arose with labour relations. Generally morale remained high following the war years, but efforts to convince staff that things would improve with nationalisation were a failure. Pay compared badly with other industries, and frequent changes of Transport Minister and national economic crises did not help. Lance's view was that there should be no 'us and them'. His motto was 'We are all railwaymen', and he worked on the principle that it was foolish to initiate any important official request unless the likely agreement of the other party had been secured. Many people admired Lance's directness and resolution, although others felt he was something of a bully in imposing his will. But he was never short of moral courage, and never shirked assuming responsibility.

Henry Johnson became the new BRB Chairman after Raymond was forced to resign by the Labour Government in 1967. It was he who had the idea of moving Lance to become the new General Manager of the Southern Region in 1968. Although at first reluctant, Lance took up this new position within weeks. His time on the Western had taught him many useful lessons during a period of reorganisation and rehabilitation, when established GWR habits were being discarded, for better of worse. He always regarded the Western as a friendly concern where there was little backbiting and much appreciation of each other's qualities.

To Lance the Southern seemed even more closely knit than the Western, and he found himself on numerous boards that collectively resembled an empire of their own. He quickly instituted the routine of Monday morning meetings. Soon he had assembled a good team, although they were always ready to tell him quite openly if they had differing views. He was, again, a 'foreigner'. But he would always listen and encourage. As one member of staff remarked, 'There was no doubting who was the Boss. Lance set an example and led from the front.' In line with his previous policy, he saw to it that he visited stations, freight depots, booking offices, locomotive depots and signal boxes, speaking to every railwayman he saw.

Looking to the future, Lance commissioned a wide-ranging report 'Southern into the Seventies', a ten-year modernisation plan that some consider his crowning glory. Taking a year to put together, it enabled the Region to see ahead and gave the BRB warning of future essential capital investment. Two years before the plan was released, he told the Board that a long-term investment scheme was essential for modernisation, but was told by the Government that this was not possible as it would tie successors to a future budget. Lance soon realised that he was in the same straitjacket as the other nationalised industries, and would have to rely on an annual budget. This was exacerbated by the fact that there were 11 Ministers of Transport between 1945 and 1970, so there simply could be no steadiness of policy. Improvements did come eventually, but slower than required and mostly after Lance's retirement.

The Southern was a much-complained-about Region, and Lance recognised that effective public relations and personal responses to criticisms would help to defuse such complaints by presenting the railway's point of view. As part of the campaign to promote the ten-year plan he invited to a meeting the 162 MPs from the SR's area; it was an excellent audio-visual presentation, but only 38 of the MPs attended.

The Southern Board held monthly lunches for businessmen, MPs and others, and it was arranged that each guest should sit between a Board member and a senior railway officer. Lance felt that this contact with prominent members of the community was a great assistance in promoting relations with the very public railway that he managed.

In preparation for his retirement, the Ibbotsons moved out of London to Waverley, near Farnham, Surrey. The new house came with 3 acres, so Lance would be able to indulge his love of gardening and vegetable-growing.

Meanwhile the Government was employing management consultants to examine the railway and find ways to halt its decline. Lance disliked this approach of 'pulling up the plants every few minutes to see how they were growing'. He did not like being interrogated by consultants, and the reorganisation and upheavals that followed. He therefore surprised his staff by deciding to retire two years early, on his birthday in February 1972, at the age of 63. His final lunch was held at the Charing Cross Hotel, with MPs and senior officers invited. A model railway was laid around the dining table; at the end of the lunch a train moved around, stopping in front of each guest, and each was then invited to take a present from a wagon. His retirement gift from the Southern Region was a fully equipped greenhouse for his garden, with running water and heating.

Sadly in the 1980s Joan's health began to fail and another move was made in May 1987 to a suitable bungalow in Winchester, to be nearer their daughter Rhona. Joan's health continued to decline, and she died in October 1989. This was a great blow to Lance, after 58 years of marriage. Lance later remarried, to an old friend, herself a widow, and they lived a happy and busy life in London. He died in Wandsworth, south London, in February 1998.

One colleague summed him up thus: 'He worked hard, he set an example, he led from the front. There was another side, too, despite the austere outer shell of the man and the impression of being hard and unfeeling to some people; I witnessed many acts of kindness by him to people, most of whom were in no position to influence things on his behalf. All in all I remember Lance with affection, for his professionalism, his industry and genuineness of purpose.'

1959

Photographed in July 1959 this is the site of Undy water troughs on the South Wales main line about 1½ miles west of Severn Tunnel Junction station – the water tank supplying the troughs, which dated from about 1906, is visible in the middle distance. An overbridge is being rebuilt, probably as a result of works to expand the west yard at Severn Tunnel Junction, behind the camera. The yard closed completely in 1987.

Top: Facing the camera during that visit is John Bickerton BEng MICE (1901-69), the District Engineer at Newport. He had taken a 1st Class Honours degree in Engineering at Liverpool University, and began his railway career in 1924 under A. P. Ross, Chief Engineer of the Cheshire Lines Committee. In 1926 he supervised the remodelling of Trafford Park Sidings. After working in Argentina and Spain, he joined the GWR's New Works Department in 1930. Among his jobs were various contracts at Bristol Temple Meads, Birmingham and Stourbridge, as well as Severn Tunnel Junction. Prior to his post at Newport, he had been District Engineer for Cardiff. He retired in 1964.

Right: Also attending at Severn Tunnel Junction on the same day were I. G. Carson and W. R. Stevens. Mr Carson (left) was Assistant to the General Manager (Works), and had worked in the GWR General Manager's office since 1925. In 1957 he became Assistant to the General Manager, concerned mainly with major works schemes being carried out under the WR's Modernisation Plan. Mr Stevens, facing the camera, had recently been made Divisional Traffic Manager for Cardiff.

A new Hafodyrynys East signal box was brought into use on Monday 26 January 1959, and is seen here in July. It stood on the former Newport, Abergavenny & Hereford Railway east of Crumlin. This rather utilitarian 'modern' design, which came into use in 1957, was known as Type 37a, but examples were nicknamed 'plywood wonders'. They were intended to be cheap and quick to erect, being made up from standard parts (there was often a door at each end of the box, whether required or not!). The wood was stained and varnished before assembly, and looked good when new. The structures were also easy to dismantle, and several served in more than one location, with further examples at Maidenhead, Twyford, Radyr and Dainton, among others; some, as here at Hafodyrynys, had slatted canopies above the windows to reduce glare.

Hafodyrynys Colliery first appears in the late 1870s. Following nationalisation in 1947, many small local collieries closed, but others, including Hafodyrynys, saw increased investment, with the old pit closed and a new one sunk, connected to Tirpentwys and Glyntillery collieries. The work was completed in 1959 at a cost of £5.5 million in anticipation of raising 800,000 tons of coal per year. As described in the excellent Northern Mine Research Society website, the new colliery buildings and washery boasted modern buildings and equipment for maximum efficiency; they had reinforced concrete frames filled with brick or glass panels, and flat, curved or waveform concrete roofs. The washery (on the right) was built of reinforced concrete with continuous glazed panels. The result can be seen here in this July 1959 view. The railway sidings had a capacity for 414 empty and 317 full (12-ton) wagons. Unfortunately the New Mine never reached its full potential and was something of a 'white elephant'. Hafodyrynys was closed in 1966, the other two following in 1968 and 1975 respectively, and the site was cleared in 1985, although the washery survives in skeletal form.

Opposite: The reason for the Swindon event may well have been the entry into service of 'Warship' Class diesel-hydraulic locomotive D810 'Cockade' on Wednesday 16 September 1959, and the locomotive is seen here in pristine condition. When the Western Region decided on the adoption of diesel-hydraulic rather than diesel-electric transmission, it was West Germany that was leading the way. Deutsche Bundesbahn's 'V200' diesel-hydraulics had been in production since 1956, and the WR negotiated a licence with their German manufacturer, Krauss-Maffei, to build a scaled-down version to suit the smaller British loading gauge. The WR locomotives were very similar in appearance, and the first 33, Nos D800-D832, were built at Swindon. Unfortunately they were not especially successful, and there was prejudice within BR against hydraulic transmission. As a result withdrawals started as early as 1968. In 1970 No D810 became the last member of the class to be still in green livery, and was taken out of service in November 1971, although quickly reinstated. It was finally withdrawn, one of the last four still at work, in December 1972, and cut up in September 1973 at Swindon Works.

Above: On the platform at Swindon in September 1959, presumably during an official visit, is, on the left, R. A. Smeddle MIMechE MILocoE (1899-1964). Robert Smeddle joined the North Eastern Railway as a pupil in 1919, and in 1925 was appointed Assistant Works Manager, Cowlairs, followed by Assistant Carriage & Wagon Works Manager at York. From 1936 to 1941 he was Locomotive Works Manager at Darlington, subsequently being appointed Mechanical Engineer, Darlington. In 1949 he moved to the Southern Region as Deputy Mechanical & Electrical Engineer. His career culminated in his appointment to the Western Region in 1951, where he became Chief Mechanical & Electrical Engineer. In 1959 he was elected President of the Institution of Mechanical Engineers, and in that year was the author of 'Dieselisation – problems, prospects and progress', a paper delivered to the WR's London Lecture & Debating Society. He retired from the WR in 1962 but unfortunately died soon afterwards. In 1955 he was instrumental in the fitting of high-degree superheaters, double blastpipes and chimneys to the 'King' and 'Castle' 4-6-0s, following trials with BR Class 8 No 71000 'Duke of Gloucester' on the Swindon stationary testing plant. He was later much associated with the introduction of diesel-hydraulic locomotives.

According to Lance's caption to the picture, the gentleman in the centre is a Mr Smith, and on the right Herr von Mittenmuller – both cannot be further identified, but perhaps the latter was a visitor from Germany, maybe a representative of Krauss-Maffei, who licensed BR to construct the WR's 'Warships'? Swindon Station East signal box can be seen in the right distance.

COCKADE
WARSHIP CLASS

Sc 51046
IMPORTANT

What became the BR Class 126 diesel multiple units were built at Swindon in 1959-60 to work services from Glasgow to Ayr, south to Girvan and Stranraer and coastal services to Largs and Ardrossan. The class comprised 22 three-car sets, and were a development of the earlier Swindon-built DMUs introduced four years earlier to work the Edinburgh Waverley-Glasgow Queen Street services. They were know as 'Inter-City' units, long before the term was used for main-line expresses.

Photographed in September 1959 is the driving compartment and part of the open saloon seating area of 'leading' Driving Motor Brake Second No SC51046. This unit entered service on 12 September and was allocated new to Ayr, initially coupled to Trailer First No SC59396 and Motor Second No SC51024. In order for the units to run as six-coach sets, the latter vehicle, known as the 'intermediate' driving car, had gangways at both ends, with a driving compartment offset to one side. The other end of the set, seen here, had the full-width cab and no gangway.

Each of the two power cars was fitted with two AEC 150hp underfloor engines with mechanical transmission and a maximum speed of 70mph. The class survived almost intact until mass withdrawals in the early 1980s. This particular vehicle was withdrawn from Ayr on 1 March 1982 and scrapped by Mayer Newman of Snailwell, Cambridgeshire, in May.

OCT 24
No. 15
D817

Opposite: The 'Warships' used hydraulic transmission coupled with lightweight alloy construction to make them substantially lighter than contemporary diesel-electric designs; for example a Type 4 'Peak' weighed just over 138 tons with eight axles, while a 'Warship' was only 78 tons on four axles. An idea of the method of construction is seen in this view of No D817, to be named 'Foxhound', in Swindon Works in September 1959. The bodyshell accommodated two 1,135hp Maybach MD650 engines coupled to Mekydro hydraulic transmission; the engines were built under licence by Bristol Siddeley at its Ansty factory, near Coventry.

No D817 entered traffic on 9 March 1960 in green livery, being repainted maroon in September 1966. Its short life of only just over 11 years ended with withdrawal on 3 October 1971; it was cut up at Swindon the following March, still in maroon, one of only a handful to have escaped repainting in BR Blue. However, the locomotive lived on in the form of a Bachmann 'Branchline' OO scale model – in maroon. Note that Sid's birthday will be celebrated on 24 October!

Right: Seen in a more advanced state on the same day is No D813 'Diadem'. This will be ready to enter service at Cardiff Canton on 9 December 1959, and was the first of the class to be fitted from new with a four-character headcode box; this feature was later retrofitted to the earlier locomotives. 'Diadem' enjoyed a slightly longer life than D817, not being withdrawn until New Year's Day 1972, and scrapped at Swindon that September.

Above: South Lambeth Goods Depot was a GWR enclave in the heart of Southern territory, located just south of the Thames, adjacent to Battersea Power Station and about a mile south of Victoria station. It was accessed from the south at Stewarts Lane Junction, and presumably involved a reversal into the curving yard, which was east of and at right angles to the Southern lines. It was laid out on the site of the reservoirs and filtration beds of the old Southwark & Vauxhall Waterworks. Lance is clearly part of an official visit to the yard – note the bowler hat! – in October 1959.

The large warehouse was built in 1911-13, the yard opening on 1 January in the latter year. The warehouse was 400 feet long, with a Hennebique reinforced-concrete frame and brick infill (Francois Hennebique [1842-1921] was a French engineer and builder who pioneered the use of reinforced concrete in the 1890s). Other buildings were added in 1928-29. Apparently most of the warehouse space was rented out and used by various companies to store their products for distribution. Eventually the site employed nearly 600 men.

Goods trains at South Lambeth came to and from the yards at Old Oak Common, Hanwell Bridge, Acton and Park Royal; at one time outward traffic for the GWR system was taken out by about 14 pilot 'trips' each day. Note the 'Conflat' wagons with containers and the Scammell 'mechanical horse'.

Opposite: This view was taken from the upper floor of the warehouse – note the large number of 'Conflats' in the yard. In the background, the first viaduct carries the former SE&CR high-level line to Brixton, avoiding the Stewarts Lane junctions. The further viaduct carries the former LB&SCR lines, south to Brixton and west towards Clapham Junction. In the top right-hand corner can be glimpsed part of Battersea Power Station. The whole area has now disappeared under the Battersea Power Station redevelopment scheme.

Left: When the GWR began construction of the Severn Tunnel in 1873, all progressed well until 16 October 1879 when the 'Great Spring' broke in, overcame the pumps and flooded the works. It happened again in 1883, which eventually led to the installation of six beam engines by Harveys of Hayle, Cornwall; they had 70-inch-diameter cylinders and a 10-foot stroke. At last the spring was brought under control, and the first official train traversed the tunnel in 1885, with passenger services beginning the following year.

The pumping engines, powered by Lancashire boilers, were installed in 1886 in a large engine house at Sudbrook, on the Welsh side of the river – indeed, it was at the time the largest such engine house in the world. It had extremely strong foundations to support the weight of the engines, and the bricks were made locally using clay excavated from the tunnel.

The six engines were still in situ until 1961, by which time only three were in steam, and these were replaced by electric pumps. Sadly, the original engines were scrapped. The 14 electric pumps, now housed in the shaft, are replaced every 30 years or so; they were replaced in the 1990s by Railtrack, and again in 2022 by Network Rail. The building is now empty, but listed.

In October 1959 the WR Board visited the engine house, perhaps as a prelude to the replacement of the beam engines. In the centre of the group is Robert Smeddle, the WR Chief Mechanical & Electrical Engineer.

Right: Lance photographed the beams during the visit; they each weighed 20 tons. There were three bucket pumps at one end of the building and three plunger pumps at the other, but only four had to be working at any one time. Some 23 to 30 million gallons are pumped out daily, normally into the adjacent river.

That same month members of the Western Area Board visited South Wales to inspect various railway installations and equipment and meet the officers of the new South Wales Divisional Traffic Organisation. As Works Assistant to the General Manager for New Projects, Lance was particularly interested to visit the new marshalling yard at Margam, and he photographed the group on the platform at Cardiff General station. The gentlemen in the front row are, from the left, F. A. Parish and P. T. Heady, Area Board Member (hat in hand); C. H. Swancutt, Station Master (in top hat); R. F. Hanks, Area Board Chairman; C. W. Rodd, Area Board member; and Sir John Carew Pole, Bart, also an Area Board member.

Opposite: Steelmaking at Port Talbot began with the Margam Iron & Steel Works in the mid-1920s, and by the 1960s the Port Talbot complex was the largest steelworks in Europe. Part of BR's Modernisation plan was to provide a number of new yards to speed up freight transit, and one of three planned for the Western Region was that at Margam, which cost £2 million and opened in 1960 (the others, at Gloucester and Shrewsbury, did not materialise). The yard would provide sorting facilities for traffic to and from the Swansea area and West Wales, and in particular traffic to and from the adjacent Steel Company of Wales plant.

A contemporary BR brochure describes the yard as 'the most up-to-date in Europe and is the first to be fully automatic in operation, making use of the latest electronic techniques, including Radar and Analogue Computers. It is capable of sorting 4,500 wagons daily and could deal with a total of 220 trains in and out each day… It occupies an area of 178 acres and comprises 33 miles of plain line… There are 12 Reception Sidings with engine release line and hump engine return line, together with 50 double-ended sorting sidings, 10 single-ended holding sidings, and 7 single-ended tranship and cripple sidings with tranship platform and cattle pens. The capacity of the Reception Sidings varies from 63 to 95 wagons plus engine and van. The shortest Sorting Siding holds 43 wagons and the longest 101.' In addition, there were 240 points and crossings.

In operation the 50 sidings were divided into 15 for the Steel Company of Wales, 23 for down traffic, 11 for up, and one for brake vans. The yard seems to be already occupied by rakes of wagons in these October 1959 photographs. The first is a view of the yard taken from the Control Tower, looking northwards towards Port Talbot and its steelworks. In the centre are sorting sidings 9 to 14, with 13 and 14 occupied; the longest sorting siding was 700 yards. Floodlighting was provided by 99 tubular steel towers 55 feet high.

Right: Operations in the yard were directed from the four-storey control tower. Stairs from the ground-floor lobby led to the first floor, which housed the relay and battery rooms, the traffic office and a workshop. On the second floor was the air-conditioning plant. The third floor contained the airy control room, its three glass walls providing a commanding view from end to end of the yard. The floors were linked by a lift.

Left: A view of the control panel. The right-hand section controlled the signalling of the Reception Sidings and associated tracks, while the left-hand portion controlled all equipment associated with the humping operations. The eastern end of each sorting siding had a red light for each occupied track circuit, equal to five wagon-lengths; this enabled the controllers to see the positions of wagons or cuts after dark or in poor visibility, useful if the vehicles had failed to travel the full predicted distance along a siding, when a shunting loco would have to be sent to finish the job. The handy central drawer contained a telephone and hand microphone.

Right: Members of the Western Area Board inspect and discuss Secondary Retarders 2 and 3.

Opposite: This is the hump, looking towards the Reception Sidings. Wagons were propelled to the top at about 1½mph then descended by gravity on a sharp gradient of 1 in 18, which flattened out to 1 in 80 through the two primary and eight secondary retarders. Note the 'humping signal' beside the track at the summit of the hump, whose indication was reproduced in the cab of the hump shunter. The River Kenfig flowed across the site so had to be diverted into straight cuts on either side of the yard, linked by a channel flowing through the reinforced concrete box culverts seen on the left passing beneath the hump.

D3435

Opposite and above: The yard shunter, No D3435, pulls a single wagon across one of the secondary retarders. This shunter, new in 1958, became Class 08 08365; it was withdrawn from Margam in September 1980 and scrapped at Swindon the following April. Eventually the yard used three shunters, Nos D3436-8, from Duffryn yard, each equipped with two-way radio telephone to communicate with the sorting sidings inspector and the control tower. The wagon was then presumably released over the hump to run across Secondary Retarder 3, the 'first wagon humped', according to Lance's note on the slide mount. The retarders were operated electro-pneumatically; the primary retarders were 72 feet long, arranged in 12-foot articulated sections. They had two sets of control valves so that each half of the retarder could be operated independently. Their main function was to maintain a gap between wagons to enable points to be changed ahead of them. The secondary retarders were 36 feet in length and had just one set of control valves. As can be seen they rested on timber foundations in a concrete pit.

The retarders were set to ensure that wagons should not buffer up to those already in a siding at more than 4mph, and as each wagon, or 'cut' of wagons, rolled down, its weight and speed were automatically assessed and its progress regulated by the retarders, using techniques very sophisticated for the time, including adjustments for wind direction and strength, all developed and produced by AEI.

8
6

An interesting photograph captured by Lance in 1959 was this cameo at Newton Abbot station. Packing of sleepers is in progress, a process described in detail by a 1947 LMS film 'Measured Shovel Packing' – and presumably a similar method to that employed throughout BR.

To detect how much a rail was out of level due to 'hanging' sleepers, three boards were clipped to the rail: the sight board, at a high spot in the rail, the intermediate board (which was adjustable for height) four or five sleepers away, and the target board. A spirit level was built into each. The ganger sat behind the sight board, and the intermediate board was lowered until its scale read zero. The ganger, looking through a slot in the sight board, aligned the yellow and black squares of the target so that the intermediate's upper edge coincided with the target's horizontal centre line. The reading of the pointer against the scale was then chalked on the rail below the intermediate board. This board was then moved four or five sleepers nearer the target and the process repeated, producing a figure at every fourth or fifth sleeper.

To estimate the amount of hollow beneath a sleeper a 'voidmeter' was used, fixed in the ballast beside the relevant sleepers. At one end there was a spring-loaded pointer, which rested on the sleeper close to, but not touching, the chair. Then the friction pointer was pushed down until its pin rested on the spring pointer.

A passing train depressed the hanging sleepers, and the spring pointer of the voidmeter moved up the scale, taking the friction pointer with it and leaving it at the highest point reached. The number of divisions between the two pointers was read, and the figure chalked on the sleeper. There was now a voidmeter figure on every hanging sleeper and a sighting board figure on the rail at each sleeper. The two figures were added together, and the result was the number of canisters of chips that must go under that sleeper; each full canister was equal to 1/16th of an inch of slack.

The ballast between the sleepers was then opened out where necessary and the bed revealed. The line was jacked up and the necessary number of canisters of chips spread evenly under each sleeper for 15 inches on either side of the rail. The rail was then lowered, and the ballast returned to 'backfill the boxing' between the sleepers. Then, when tested again with a voidmeter, no slack at all should be recorded.

The picture shows canisters of chips from a barrow being passed down to the ganger on the track serving Platform 6. No high-vis jackets in 1959!

1960

Opposite: In February 1960 Lance was back at Margam, which was all but complete. This general view from the Control Tower is looking south, with the Reception Sidings in the distance. There were 12 of these, flanked on the left by the Up Departure Road and Engine Release Road, and on the right by the Down Through line, glimpsed on the extreme right of the picture passing behind the Control Tower. Sidings 8 to 12 (on the left of the set in this view) were for up trains, while the remainder were accessible from both directions. Between sidings 7 and 8 was the Humper Return Road, allowing the shunting loco to regain the tail of the next train of wagons to be propelled over the hump. The culverted River Kenfig flows beneath the bridge in the middle distance, and beyond it is the main Amenity Block. A 'cut' of wagons appears to be in the process of being humped, passing over Primary Retarder 1, perhaps for the benefit of the visitors.

Above: A close-up of the Amenity Block, which contained offices for the Yardmaster and his staff, and storage accommodation. The upper floor housed a fully equipped kitchen and mess room. Lined up outside is a fine array of 1950s cars.

Top: Inside the Amenity Block Lance photographed some of his colleagues, apparently in the mess room area. On the right is W. R. Stevens, Divisional Traffic Manager for Cardiff. On the left is J. F. M. (Frank) Taylor, District Traffic Superintendent, Swansea. New chairs and tables are stacked up in the background ready for use.

Bottom: Here are the Reception Sidings on the Control Panel. The BR brochure tells us that 'a key switch is used at each signal position at the entrance to a route, and a push button at the exit, to select the particular route required. On a route being set up, the points are automatically set to the required position, after which the representation of that route on the panel is lit by a line of white lights and the signal is cleared… As the train enters the route, track occupancy is indicated by the section of route indication lights being changed from white to red.'

Opposite: At the north (Port Talbot) end of the 50 sorting sidings was the 92-lever Margam Sorting Sidings signal box, a larger version of the 'plywood wonder' already seen at Hafodyrynys. The bridge carries a line linking the Steel Company of Wales's Abbey South Sidings and Grange Coke Ovens (off to the left) with the Port Talbot Railway & Docks's Ogmore Vale Extension line towards Tondu, as well as the Up Arrival line round the west side of the Sorting Sidings and thence to the Reception Sidings. The lines off to the left lead from the marshalling yard to the SCoW's works. Ahead the tracks join the goods lines of the South Wales main line at Margam Abbey Works East signal box. Sorting Sidings box closed in 1987, but stood derelict until the early 2010s before being demolished.

Opposite: The Yard was officially opened on Monday 11 April 1960 by British Transport Commission Member and Western Region General Manager Keith Grand, and Lance was there with many other interested parties, who appear to have arrived by road coach. In this view of the Control Tower, the open-ended building houses the stand-by generator and compressor plant supplying air to the pneumatic retarders and points.

Above: A cut of wagons carrying cable drums rolls from the hump into one of the Sorting Sidings. Unfortunately, the imminent decline of wagonload traffic and the advent of block trains and Freightliner services rendered such yards increasingly redundant. Margam's planned throughput was never fully achieved; a year after opening the yard was operating at half capacity, dealing with 60 to 70 trains, representing an average of 2,250 wagons per day. Around 30% of the wagons were for the adjacent steel works. As a result the hump yard closed in 1980, to be replaced by a smaller 'knuckle' yard with a smaller hump.

THE LAST STEAM LOCO
"EVENING
BUILT IN SWINDON WORKS AND NAMED ON MA
92220

Opposite: Friday 18 March 1960 was a momentous day in the history of Swindon Works when Class 9F No 92220 'Evening Star' was named at a special ceremony. The engine stood in the Works in front of a curtain bearing the words 'The last steam locomotive to be built by British Railways – "Evening Star" – Built in Swindon and named on March 18th 1960'. The name was chosen by a competition run in late 1959 by the BR Western Region Staff Magazine, offering a prize of 10 guineas. Although the last to be built, the engine was not the last 9F numerically, as Crewe Works had already completed engines with higher numbers (Nos 92221-92250). Mounting the platform are railway dignitaries and the Mayor of Swindon, Alderman F. D. Jefford.

'Evening Star' was the only British main-line steam locomotive to be earmarked for preservation as soon as it was built. After a career of only five years and one day, it was withdrawn in March 1965 following a minor shunting accident, and became part of the National Collection at York Railway Museum.

Top: Making a speech is Reginald F. Hanks MIMechE (1896-1976), Chairman of the BTC's Western Area Board since 1955. Perhaps ironically, although having trained in engineering at Swindon Works, Mr Hanks had been a Director of Morris Motors and the British Motor Corporation since 1947. He said, 'In many ways it is an emotional occasion, not to say a sad one, but it is also a very great day for Swindon, and a proud day for Great Western men everywhere, who will find much satisfaction, since there had to be "a last one", that it should fall to the lot of Swindon to see the job through.'

He went on to say, 'Although it is not of the Great Western family, Swindon has done its best to make up for that "deficiency" by dollying the engine up in Great Western colours and by conferring upon it the halo or crown of Swindon – "that mystical copper cap to her chimney".'

Bottom: The actual naming was done by Keith Grand (1900-83), former Assistant General Manager of the GWR, later General Manager and Chief Regional Officer of BR's Western Region, and a BTC member. Liverpool-born, he had joined the GWR in 1919 after leaving Rugby School. The WR Staff Magazine reported that a 'resounding cheer' echoed through "A" Shop when Mr Grand 'drew aside the curtain revealing the name…' Also on the platform were the Mayoress of Swindon, Assistant General Manager Mr H. G. Bowles, and Robert Smeddle, Chief Mechanical & Electrical Engineer, nearest the camera.

There were other things to see and celebrate at Swindon Works on that day, including former GWR railcar No 4, already in preservation. It was built by the GWR in 1934, one of three (Nos 2-4) fitted with a buffet counter, intended for use as an express businessmen's service between Birmingham and Cardiff. The buffet served hot and cold drinks and wines and a small amount of hot food and snacks. Coffee and milk were heated by a gas boiler, while a small toilet had hot water heated by the engines' exhausts. The underframes and the two 8.85-litre diesel engines were built at AEC, with the bodies constructed by Park Royal; No 4 is the only example to survive with the earlier design of streamlined 'flying banana' bodywork. They were 60ft 6in long and had a top speed of 80mph.

These units ran into the early 1960s, and in 1963 No 4 found itself in the apprentice training school at Swindon Works. It was later suggested that it be retained for display at the town's Great Western Railway Museum, and meanwhile was placed in storage at the former Hellifield loco shed. In 1966 it entered the custodianship of Swindon Corporation, then by 1970 was leased to Didcot Railway Centre. In 1975, when the NRM at York opened, it moved there as part of the National Collection.

Top: Inside the Works is brand-new 'Warship' No D818 'Glory', which went on to have a somewhat controversial career. The locomotive entered service on 30 March 1960, less than a fortnight after this picture was taken in 'A' Shop. After a service life of only 12 years it was withdrawn on 1 November 1972, but remained at Swindon for about as many years again. It was repainted from Rail Blue with full yellow ends back into its original green livery and was presumed to be intended for preservation, making an appearance at several open days. However, in 1985 it was announced that Swindon Works was to close. Some consider that it was as a result of this unpopular news that 'Glory' was unceremoniously cut up in November of that year.

D818 had been used as a source of spares for sister loco No D832 'Onslaught', which unlike 'Glory' was one of just two 'Warships' to survive into preservation. Indeed, between 2020 and 2022 on the East Lancashire Railway 'Onslaught' was renumbered and renamed 818 'Glory' in tribute to its lost sister – 'the one that got away'.

Bottom: In steam outside the Works was, appropriately, Hawksworth 'Castle' Class 4-6-0 No 7007 'Great Western'. When built in July 1946 the engine carried the name 'Ogmore Castle', but nationalisation loomed and its was realised that No 7007 was the last express passenger locomotive to have been built by the GWR. In January 1948, therefore, it was renamed – note the company's coat of arms under the nameplate. First allocated to Wolverhampton Stafford Road shed, it later moved to Old Oak Common then Worcester, where it stayed for 13 years before withdrawal in February 1963. It was scrapped at Cashmore's, Great Bridge, in January 1964.

A little-photographed corner of the Works was the laundry in No 10 Shop in the Carriage & Wagon Works, with its all-female staff.

Top: This delightful cameo was captured in Bridgnorth High Street, Shropshire, in April 1960. The gentleman on the left is Armand Cardani, the Western Region's Chief Signal & Telegraph Engineer. He appears to be purchasing ice creams for the group, with small blocks in his left hand and wafers in his right.

Born in 1921, he joined the LNER's S&T Department in 1938 and, following an apprenticeship, was appointed as an engineering graduate. His main work was in connection with the Great Eastern electrification, and this continued until 1947 when he joined the GWR. He became Assistant Signal Engineer of the Western Region in 1957 and in 1959, at the age of 38, became the Region's youngest Chief S&T Engineer. In 1959 he wrote 'Multiple Aspect Signalling, British practice' for the Institution of Railway Signal Engineers, and by 1968 had overseen the conversion of more than 1,000 track miles of the WR to multiple-aspect signalling. He was also involved in the railway alterations for the Margam Strip Mill scheme.

In 1968 he transferred to the London Midland Region in the same role, and in 1975 was appointed as BR Director of S&T Engineering, a post he held until his retirement in 1981. He joined the Institution of Railway Signal Engineers as a student in 1942, was on the Council by 1960 and became President in 1970. On his death in 2002 the IRSE wrote, 'We are grateful for all that he has done and we will miss his leadership, guidance, friendship and unfailing good humour.'

The other two gentlemen are I. G. Carson, Assistant to the General Manager, and a Mr Griffiths.

Bottom: Probably on the same day Lance photographed the distinctive frontage of Kidderminster station, which opened with the extension of the Oxford, Worcester & Wolverhampton Railway from Worcester to Stourbridge in 1852. It passed to the West Midland Railway in 1860, which amalgamated with the GWR in 1863.

The original station building was replaced in 1859, then in 1863 that was destroyed by fire. The third building is seen here, built in a mock-Tudor style. This survived until 1968, when dry rot led to its demolition and replacement by a more utilitarian brick building. This in turn was replaced by a larger and more suitable glass-fronted building, which opened in June 2020.

This is not to be confused with the late-Victorian-style Kidderminster Town station of the heritage Severn Valley Railway, which opened on an adjacent site in 1984.

Opposite: The Esso oil refinery at Milford Haven was opened on 3 November 1960 by Prince Philip, Duke of Edinburgh. It was served by a jetty that was started in 1957 and is seen here still under construction in April 1960. It extended 1,200 yards into the Milford Haven Waterway in order to reach water deep enough for the super-tankers of the day. The refinery had the capacity to process 4.5 million tons of crude oil per year.

Although it didn't open fully until November, the first oil tanker to arrive was the 36,000-ton 'Esso Portsmouth' on 8 July. Unfortunately, almost as soon as she began to discharge her cargo of crude oil one of the delivery arms fractured and a serious spillage took place. The oil ignited, causing a massive explosion, and although most of the cargo was saved, the tanker was seriously damaged. The vast majority of the refinery's production was sent out by ship, but it was rail connected and trains carrying liquefied gas were sent to the Midlands and Scotland.

The refinery closed in March 1983 and today the site is used as a Liquid Natural Gas terminal owned by Exxonmobile, served by huge LNG tankers arriving from Qatar.

Right: Seen at Milford Haven is, on the left, Frank Taylor, District Traffic Superintendent, Swansea; the other gentleman is unidentified. Note the cars of the day, including in the centre background a Ford Zephyr estate.

Left: The GWR's locomotive shed at Landore, Swansea, was built in 1932. By 1959 the shed's allocation was 68 locomotives, including main-line 'Castles' and 'Halls' as well as freight engines, but it closed in June 1961, to be replaced by a purpose-built diesel depot in 1963. Just over a year before closure, in April 1960, this was the view looking north towards the shed yard from the turntable, with the main shed building on the left and the coaling stage on the right. The shed was squeezed into the 'V' of tracks diverging from Landore Junction, the West Wales main line off to the left and the Swansea branch behind the coal stage. The two locos in this slightly forlorn view – brightened only by the shiny Swansea-registered Morris Minor – are unidentified, but the near one is probably one of the five '56xx' 0-6-2Ts allocated to the shed and recorded by a trainspotter on 17 April 1960.

Opposite: The Landore visit was made by the Works & Equipment Committee, and here we see two eminent railwaymen, apparently discussing the finer points of the valve gear of a 9F 2-10-0. It seems that Landore never had a 9F allocation, so this must have been a visiting locomotive; the anonymous traïnspotter mentioned above recorded Banbury-allocated No 92232 during the month of this visit, so perhaps this is it.

On the left in the bowler hat is Frederick William Hawksworth (1884-1976), former Chief Mechanical Engineer of the GWR, a post he continued to hold after the formation of British Railways. He continued to work on locomotive design until his retirement at the end of 1949. Hawksworth never married and died in 1976, aged 92, having enjoyed a long retirement. A Freeman of the Borough of Swindon since 1960, his ashes were interred at St Mark's Church (the 'Railway Church'), Swindon, where he had been a lifelong member of the choir.

Beside him is Roland Curling Bond (1903-80). Born in Ipswich, Bond was apprenticed to Fowler at Derby in the 1920s. After a time at the Vulcan Foundry, he returned to the LMS in 1931, and at nationalisation became Chief Officer (Locomotive Construction & Maintenance). When the Railway Executive was abolished in 1953, Bond was appointed CME, BR Central Staff, and General Manager, BR Workshops, in 1965. He retired in 1970 but, like Hawksworth, maintained a keen interest in locomotive matters. He died in Maidenhead in 1980 at the age of 77.

Staying in South Wales, in the early 1960s Port Talbot station was being rebuilt as an island platform, and this April 1960 view shows the temporary station in use while work progresses on a new island on the right. The view is looking southwards, with the famous steelworks on the right. In the middle distance, by the footbridge, is a level crossing and, on the left, the goods shed.

As part of the works Port Talbot General Middle signal box was closed and a new one built opposite (the word 'General' was dropped from the new box's title, having also been removed from the station's name in 1947). The gates were also replaced by full barriers. Note that the new box is one of the 'plywood wonders' encountered earlier at Hafodyrynys, and was only temporary until superseded by the Port Talbot panel signal box and colour light signalling, brought into use in 1963.

Top: The next three pictures were taken inside Swindon Works in May 1960. The era of the Works as a major locomotive building centre was coming to an end. On the left are 'Warship' diesel-hydraulics being built, but there are still steam locomotives in for service and repair, seen in different states of dismantlement in the background. An enthusiast visiting the Works in February 1960 managed to see almost 50 steam locomotives there, as well as half a dozen 'Warships' and five diesel shunters under construction – but outside were more than 90 steam locomotives, many destined for scrapping. Building of new main-line locos ceased in 1964 with No D1029 'Western Legionnaire', and steam was eliminated from the WR at the end of the following year.

Bottom: The Works' Machine Shop.

Opposite: Alongside the 'Warships' new lightweight diesel shunters were being built at Swindon, albeit designed to handle a kind of traffic that was rapidly declining as the Beeching upheavals took effect. Here are the frames of what would become No D2152. Brake gear is in place, together with the jackshaft on the right, beneath the cab end, which transferred the power from the Gardner 204hp eight-cylinder 8L3 engine through a Wilson-Drewry gearbox to coupling rods connecting the driving wheels. A Gardner engine is seen behind, awaiting installation.

Happily Lance photographed a locomotive that is still with us today. It was modified in 1974 when its cab was cut down to enable it to pass under low bridges on the Burry Port & Gwendraeth Valley mineral line in South Wales. Withdrawn in October 1983 as Class 03 No 03152, it was privately preserved, one of 56 to be saved from the 230 built at Swindon and Doncaster.

In 1954 the Pullman Car Company was acquired by the British Transport Commission, and with the aim of increasing dieselisation under the 1955 Modernisation Plan the BTC decided to exploit the Pullman image by commissioning a series of luxury diesel multiple unit trains to run between important business centres. Therefore in 1957 two six-car units, all 1st Class, were ordered for the London Midland Region, and three eight-car units for the WR, all built by Metro-Cammell in Birmingham. The first set undertook trials in October 1959, and the 'Midland Pullman' entered service in July 1960, followed by the WR units on 12 September, operating on weekdays only.

One of the WR units is seen brand-new at Swindon in May 1960, resplendent in its 'Nanking blue' livery with the Pullman coat of arms on the front (replaced in 1966 by full yellow warning panels). The WR's 'Birmingham Pullman' ran from Wolverhampton to Paddington, then Paddington to Birmingham Snow Hill and back, before returning to Wolverhampton in the evening. The 'Bristol Pullman' ran from Bristol to Paddington and return twice a day. From 1961 an additional morning train, the 'South Wales Pullman', ran from Paddington to Cardiff and Swansea. After 1967 the LMR sets were eventually transferred to the WR, and different service patterns were introduced, but declining reliability and increasing unpopularity saw the last sets eventually withdrawn in May 1973.

This page: Sir George Herbert Dowty (1901-75) founded Dowty Aviation in the 1930s, producing aircraft components such as hydraulic systems; the latter technology was later incorporated in his company's 'Dowty retarder' for use in railway marshalling yards. We have already met 'clasp'-type retarders at Margam, but BR tests proved that only about 30% of wagons correctly buffered up to existing stock in sidings, the rest approaching too fast or stopping short. This new system controlled wagon speeds over virtually their whole journey through the yard by means of hydraulic devices dispersed along the rails, which could either retard or accelerate wheels passing over them. The system was patented and trialled in 1959, and was announced to the world in the 'Railway Gazette' of 13 May 1960.

The following month Lance and his colleagues visited Dowty's plant beside the former Midland Railway line at Ashchurch, Gloucestershire, to see the hydraulic wagon control equipment in action, which used high-pressure oil and a system of valves. By the mid-1960s the equipment had been installed at yards in Hull, Goodmayes, Tinsley and Bescot.

The building glimpsed on the left was originally a Midland Railway horse provender stores. By the 1930s it was being used by the Cotswold Packing Co for packing fruit from the nearby Vale of Evesham, and was then occupied by Bird's Custard until acquired by Dowty in 1941. By the end of 1962 this siding had become the site of the Dowty Railway Preservation Society.

Later in June 1960 Lance headed to the Wolverhampton area, via Banbury, where he took the opportunity to photograph the recently rebuilt and modernised station. The rebuilding had been completed in 1958. Known as Banbury General until 1966 (to distinguish it from the town's Merton Street station), before rebuilding it boasted an overall roof, but this became increasing dilapidated and was demolished in 1950. The architect of the new station was Howard Cavanagh (1910-60), who was appointed as Assistant Architect to the GWR in 1947, and Architect to the Western Region following nationalisation. In 1956 he was involved in the redesign of Plymouth station, but died in an accident before its completion.

The new Banbury station had six numbered platforms, consisting of two islands with bays; today it has just the two islands, with platforms numbered 1 to 4. In the down bay at the north end of the station, then platform No 2, stands Banbury-allocated 'Hall' Class 4-6-0 No 5989 'Cransley Hall'; this was withdrawn from Neath shed in July 1962 and scrapped early the following year.

Lance and his colleagues paid a visit to Wolverhampton's Stafford Road locomotive works, and are seen here in the 1932-built Erecting Shop. Between 1859 and 1908 the works had built nearly 800 engines, but in the latter year the GWR decided to concentrate locomotive building at Swindon, so thereafter Stafford Road undertook overhauls and heavy repairs. By the 1950s Swindon was very much involved in the building of the new diesel-hydraulic locomotives, so Stafford Road Works dealt with an increasing amount of steam locomotive maintenance work. In 1959 alone 310 locomotives and 183 boilers were repaired, some of which are seen here ranged along the right-hand side of the shop. At first staff were reassured that the Works would become a main-line diesel repair depot, and their jobs were safe, but in 1963 the facility passed to the LMR. In early 1964 the last locomotive was outshopped and the Works closed in June 1964, making 500 men redundant.

Outside the Works Lance took this photograph of a Neals MC975 mobile crane with a magnet, loading scrap metal into a wagon. It is not known if the crane was taking part in a demonstration or just going about its daily work, although it looks shiny and new! The firm of R. H. Neal was established in the 1920s, and in 1930 began to manufacture mobile cranes, opening a factory in Grantham in 1937. The company was taken over by Coles Cranes in 1959, at which time it was producing a range of popular diesel-mechanical cranes with capacities up to 25 tons.

A little south of Stafford Road Works, at the end of the former GWR Victoria Basin branch from Stafford Road Junction, was Herbert Street goods station, also on the agenda for that day's visit. Built by the Shrewsbury & Birmingham Railway and opened in 1858, it was originally used as a break-of-gauge transhipment depot until the railway got its own access to Birmingham via the Birmingham, Wolverhampton & Dudley Railway, after which the line became just a goods branch. The railway/canal interchange with the Birmingham Canal at Victoria Basin was the largest such facility in the area. The goods shed seen here was built by the GWR in 1935, and on the platform is the usual variety of crates and packages typical of the wagon-load era. Note also the mobile crane on the right.

The size of Herbert Street goods station is evident in this view outside in the yard, which is full of Scammell 'mechanical horse' tractor units and trailers. The depot closed in 1972 and was later used by the old-established Carvers Building Supplies company until the premises were severely damaged by a fire in February 2012.

In 1957 the WR introduced DMUs to operate Birmingham area suburban and local services and a new diesel depot was built at Tyseley. This internal view from June 1960 highlights Derby-built Motor Brake Second vehicle No W50073, which was allocated new to Tyseley in 1957. In 1963 it transferred to the LMR together with the depot and, after some years at Cricklewood in the 1970s, returned to Tyseley in 1980. Renumbered 53073 in 1983 and given blue and grey livery, it was not withdrawn from Tyseley until October 1992, some 32 years after this photograph was taken, and subsequently scrapped – but surely having represented good value for money!

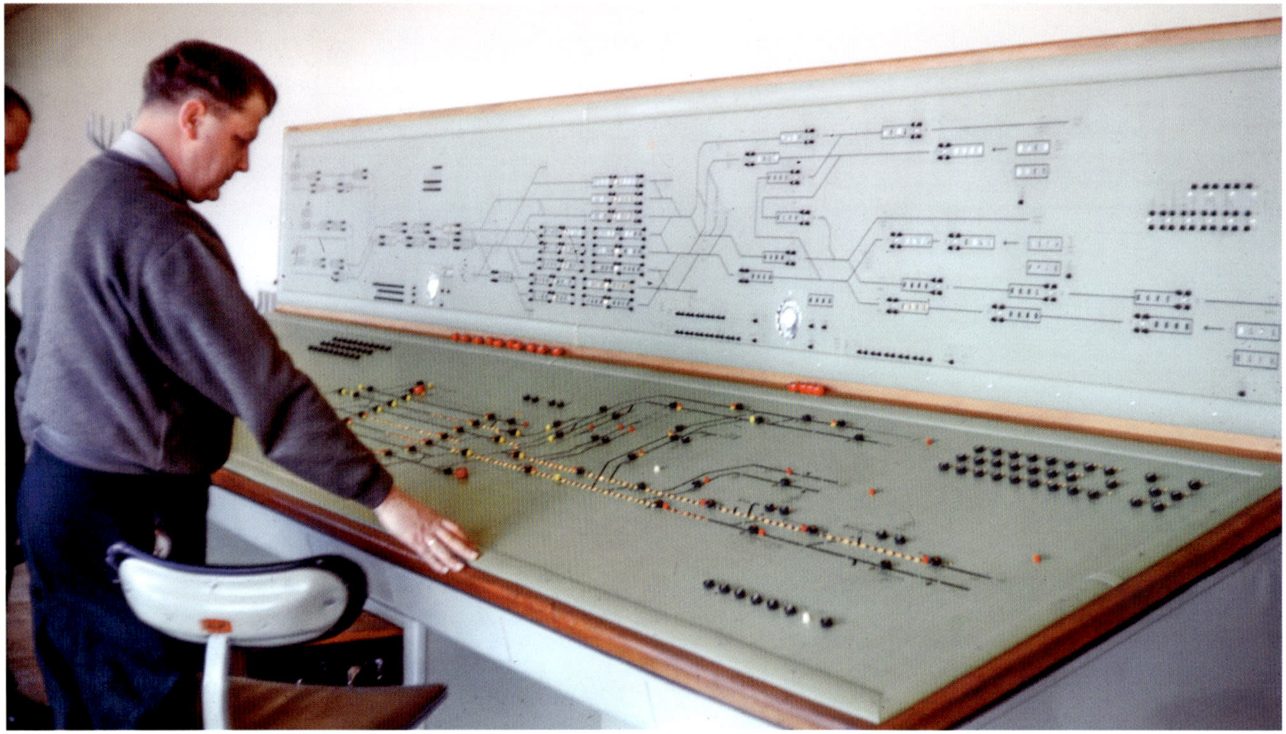

A BR(WR) Notice dated 12 November 1960 stated: 'Between the hours of 4 p.m. on Saturday, 26th November and 6 a.m. on Monday, 28th November, 1960 the Signal Engineer will be engaged upon bringing into use a new multiple aspect signalling scheme, together with a centralised signal box and control panel at Plymouth.' This new box would replace six mechanical signal boxes: East and West boxes at the station (183 and 63 levers respectively), Cornwall Junction (39 levers), Devonport Junction (31), Devonport Albert Road (29) and Lipson Junction (35), as well as 20 signalmen in each 24 hours.

The new 'panel' signal box was located at the west end of the new Platform 1 at Plymouth (now no longer known as 'North Road'). It was not the Region's first such installation, but was the first to control a considerable length of main line, from Aish in the east to St Germans in the west. Panels at Margam Yard and Birmingham Snow Hill had opened earlier in 1960, but only controlled the lines within those confines.

The route-setting console, seen here during an official visit in March 1961, was a 'Domino Integra' entrance-exit example supplied, like others on the WR, by Henry Williams Ltd of Darlington. Although extended several times during the 1970s and modified in 2024, it remains in use today, the oldest power box in the country. Although not clear from the photograph, the panel is made up of square 'Domino' tiles, patented by the Swiss Integra company. Each Domino is 40mm square and contains a small section of the layout, such as a signal or a set of points. Above the console is the duplicate track layout, displaying the four-character train descriptions. Improved train working and reduction of delays through the station resulted.

The rebuilding and modernisation of Plymouth station was interrupted by the second World War, but construction resumed in 1956. The most prominent new feature was 'Intercity House', an 11-storey tower block housing the District Manager's staff. At 47.2 metres high, it was one of the tallest buildings in the city. It was designed by architect Howard Cavanagh, who had been appointed Assistant Architect of the GWR in 1947, becoming BR Western Region Architect upon nationalisation. He worked on the Plymouth building with Ian J. Campbell, but died in a boating accident before it was completed.

Seen here looking east along Platform 2 in March 1961, the office block is under construction. The rebuilt station and tower block were officially opened by Dr Beeching a year later. In 2017 there were plans to demolish the building as part of an improved 'gateway to the city', but in 2019 Network Rail leased it for 150 years to the University of Plymouth as a new teaching facility to train nurses, midwives and other health professionals, and it has been renamed 'Intercity Place'.

Laira diesel depot also opened in March 1962 (although parts had been in use since 1960), and the main shed is seen here under construction in March of the previous year. The WR's diesel-hydraulic locomotives made their debut in 1958 and were at first accommodated in the steam shed, but that year Laira marshalling yard was closed to make room for the new depot, which was intended to undertake servicing and heavy maintenance of the new fleet. Built of reinforced concrete, it was well-lit and roomy, and comprised three adjoining buildings; here, the elevated floor is designed to allow for under-track inspection pits.

The second view shows the clean and modern-looking lavatories (yet note the overhead pull-chain cisterns!), and the third is the messroom.

The Institution of Locomotive Engineers was founded in 1911, its purpose being 'the dissemination of information concerning locomotive engineering and its allied sciences…' In May 1961 the organisation's Golden Jubilee was marked by an exhibition of locomotives and other rolling stock held in the goods yard at Marylebone station between the 11th and the 14th, and Lance recorded these three exhibits.

First we see Midland Railway Compound 4-4-0 No 1000. Built in 1902, the locomotive was withdrawn in 1951 and preserved. In 1959 it was restored to its 1914 condition, in Midland maroon livery. It hauled enthusiasts' specials for a time before being placed in Clapham Transport Museum. It has steamed since, but is now on static display at the Barrow Hill Roundhouse, on loan from the National Railway Museum, York. Just glimpsed behind it is the front of 'A4' 'Pacific' No 60022 'Mallard'. Other steam locos present were BR 8P No 71000 'Duke of Gloucester' (see below) and the youngster 9F No 92220 'Evening Star', a mere 14 months old!

Note that the banner is mounted on the yard's 35-ton Goliath electric travelling crane. This may have been a private official visit, as there is no sign of the large crowds of visitors seen in other photographs of the event!

One of the more interesting locomotives on display was the unique prototype English Electric gas turbine 4-6-0 No GT3, built at the Vulcan Foundry at Newton-le-Willows in 1961 (Gas Turbines 1 and 2 were the experimental Brown, Boveri No 18000 and the Metropolitan-Vickers No 18100.) As can be seen, externally it looked like a squared-off conventional steam locomotive, although it had a fully enclosed cab, and the tender carried kerosene fuel. It had a designed maximum speed of 90mph and weighed 123½ tons. It was painted in a Beech Leaf Brown livery, and was consequently nicknamed 'The Chocolate Zephyr' by enthusiasts. The underframes, grilles, front access doors and cab doors were painted Brunswick Green, with lettering and lining in orange.

After testing in North Wales, No GT3 moved to the former GCR shed at Leicester for testing and crew training between Leicester, Woodford Halse and eventually Marylebone. Despite being deemed a success, further finance was not forthcoming to develop the concept, and No GT3 was returned to English Electric at the Vulcan Foundry at the end of 1962. After a period in store it was partially dismantled before being finally scrapped at Ward's yard at Salford.

Beyond can be seen the front of electric locomotive No E3059, which entered traffic in July 1961, was withdrawn from service in 1990, and scrapped in 1992. Other non-steam types on display included a WR 'Hymek' and 'Warship', a Derby-built 'Peak', and 'Deltic' No D9003.

Another unique exhibit was BR Standard Class 8 'Pacific' No 71000 'Duke of Gloucester'. Designed by Robert Riddles, it was built at Crewe in 1954 as a more powerful development of the BR 'Britannia' 4-6-2s. It was unusual in being fitted with three sets of the relatively newly developed British Caprotti valve gear, the unusual arrangement of rotary operating rods clearly seen in this picture. It was first sent to Willesden shed in London where it was exhibited as part of the 16th International Railway Congress, whose Honorary President at the time was Prince Henry, Duke of Gloucester (1900-74), and No 71000 was named in his honour.

Throughout its short life of only eight years, based at Crewe North shed, it gained a reputation for poor steaming and high coal consumption, and was consequently unpopular with crews. Withdrawn at the end of 1962, 'the Duke' had been listed for preservation as part of the National Collection, but sadly that decision was later reversed, and the engine ended up at Woodham's scrapyard at Barry in 1967. There it languished for seven years until the rusting, incomplete hulk was rescued by a group of self-styled 'hopeless optimists'. Incredibly, 13 years later, in 1986, the locomotive had been restored to its as-built condition, incorporating improvements that have transformed its performance. It is currently being overhauled to return it to operational condition.

Above the locomotive can be seen the chimney and some of the wooden cooling towers of Grove Road Power Station (1902-69).

Another panel signal box similar to that at Plymouth was at Port Talbot, seen here under construction in June 1961; it opened in September 1963. This panel controlled the South Wales Main Line between Llanharan and Pembrey, including the Swansea District Line and the goods yards at Margam. In the foreground is Oakwood Road level crossing, whose barriers will be controlled from a pedestal at the west end of the signal box. The road was later diverted via a flyover at the other end of the station, and when a new station footbridge opened in 2016 the crossing closed completely.

The box had a markedly modern appearance, with its steel-framed operating floor and windows projecting towards the tracks and the road. The third box to have occupied this site (see also page 51), it has itself now been decommissioned; it closed in 2020, the area now being controlled from the South Wales Regional Operations Centre at Cardiff.

Left: Captured during an unidentified official visit in June 1961 is Brigadier Charles Ardagh Langley, who was Chief Inspecting Officer in the Railway Inspectorate from 1958 to 1963. Born in Cork, Ireland, in 1897, he was educated at the Royal Military Academy, Woolwich. He served in the Great War and was commissioned in the Royal Engineers in 1915, where he was awarded the Military Cross and Bar. He subsequently undertook higher military engineer training, including time at the Railway Training Centre, Longmoor, in the 1920s. From 1927 to 1933 he was seconded to the Great Indian Peninsular Railway in connection with the electrification of the Bombay-Poona main line. He was at Longmoor again from 1933 to 1938, then became Chief Instructor of Railways at the War Office. Following extensive service during the Second World War he was appointed Commandant of the Transportation Training Centre at Longmoor in 1946, becoming Inspecting Officer of Railways, 1946-58, then Chief Inspecting Officer, 1958-63. He reported on several significant railway accidents, including Milton (1955), Lewisham and Chapel-en-le-Frith (1957), and Hitchin (1959). He retired from BR in 1963, and died in 1987.

Opposite: This atmospheric shot shows Cardiff Canton loco shed, west of Cardiff General station, in June 1961, just over a year before steam was ousted here by diesels. It was opened by the GWR in 1882 as a six-road shed, later enlarged with a square 'roundhouse' containing a turntable from which radiated 28 roads. In the foreground is No 90579, a Vulcan Foundry-built 'Austerity' 2-8-0 of 1943. This was a Canton engine for most of its career until September 1962, when the depot was closed to steam. It was withdrawn from Staveley Barrow Hill in February 1965, and scrapped in July. In the right background is BR 'Britannia' 'Pacific' No 70020 'Mercury', built at Crewe in 1951. An Old Oak Common engine until 1956, it then moved to Canton until transferred to the London Midland Region in September 1961. It was withdrawn from Carlisle Kingmoor in January 1967, and scrapped in May 1968.

90579
90579

Opposite: Planning for a new steelworks at Llanwern began in 1956, and building started in late 1959 on grassland and wetland south of the South Wales main line between Newport and Severn Tunnel Junction. Costing a huge £150 million, the steelworks were officially opened by the Queen on 25 October 1962. In connection with the works a new arrangement of tracks was implemented near the hamlet of Llandevenny, west of Bishton and Llanwern.

In 1941 the main line here had been quadrupled, with the outer two lines as relief lines and the main lines between them. However, the up relief line needed to be on the south, Llanwern, side of the formation to serve the steelworks, so the relief and main lines west of Bishton were paired, achieved by having the new up relief line carried from the south to the north side of the formation by means of a 14-span flyover, to avoid a flat crossing with conflicting movements.

This picture, taken from the flyover in June 1961, is looking east towards Magor and Severn Tunnel Junction. The DMU is on the up main line, and beside it are the truncated remains of the original up relief, which is now on the extreme left descending from the flyover. The down relief, on the right, has been slewed around the viaduct, its original course marked by the lifted sleepers.

Right: This photograph, apparently taken from the rear of the departing inspection coach, is looking west towards Newport. The down relief line is curving round the flyover on the left, and the remains of the original up relief are on the right. Note the clever positioning of the supports to accommodate the extreme skew of the bridge.

The steelworks is now much reduced in size and scope, and Severn Tunnel Junction yard closed in 1987, so Bishton flyover is now redundant apart from occasional use by enthusiasts' specials. It has been suggested that it be removed to increase the speed and capacity of the four lines.

Hockley Goods Depot in Birmingham was located alongside the GWR main line between Wolverhampton and Snow Hill, just north of Hockley No 2 tunnel. It opened in the mid-1850s and handled both broad gauge and standard gauge traffic, becoming the principal GWR goods station for general traffic in the Birmingham area. By the early 1900s Hockley had two large sheds, Inwards and Outwards; Inwards was at the south (Birmingham) end of the yard, and Outwards towards the north. This view, from June 1961, is possibly looking north along Platforms 1 and 2, the glazed roof providing plenty of daylight. Although seemingly long past its bustling heyday, the picture provides an evocative reminder of goods handling in the wagon-load era. The mobile crane on the left, No 957, is possibly a Ransomes & Rapier product, which would be used to handle heavy items, and could also carry them between wagon and road vehicle. The yard closed in 1967.

1962

Lance had already visited the new Plymouth station in 1961 (see page 62), but he's back in March 1962 for the official opening of the newly constructed facility. These two views show the new airy concourse with its clerestory roof, clearly marked ticket windows and smart marble fascia. The ticket office was equipped with modern mechanised ticket printing and accounting machines. To the right of the ticket windows was the luxurious 'Brunel Bar', with a counter front depicting historical GWR events.

The second picture shows the waiting area (with benches also in marble) and the Enquiries office beyond. There's no explanation as to what the 'Guide A-D' signs signify – perhaps there were guided tours of the new station? Traditionalist architectural critic and poet John Betjeman was not over-impressed; in his introduction to 'The Book of the Great Western' he wrote 'Plymouth (North Road), dullest of stations and no less dull now it has been rebuilt in copybook contemporary.' It has a similar modern look to the new Coventry station, also opened in 1962.

'Intercity House', the tower block adjoining the station, housed the District Manager's staff. The first photograph shows the drawing office in the era before computer-aided design; sadly it's not possible to identify the drawings in the foreground. The second view is the District Control Office.

Left: The station was officially opened on 26 March 1962 by Dr Richard Beeching, BRB Chairman. Giving a speech here on the red carpet is Reginald Hanks, Chairman of the BTC's Western Area Board. Standing behind his right shoulder is Dr Beeching. In this rather dark photo it's not possible to positively identify the other officials, although the gentleman on the left, holding a top hat, is possibly the station master.

Opposite: A year after his first visit to Laira diesel depot (see page 64), Lance is back on an official visit to the completed facility, which fully opened on 13 March 1962 (possibly the date of this picture). The maintenance shed is seen here; Laira was one of two depots built by BR(W) for the heavy maintenance of diesels, the other being Cardiff Canton. Each of the two 300-foot roads had two berths, two for heavy and two for light maintenance.

On the left is 'Warship' No D815 'Druid'; completed in January 1960 and immediately allocated to Laira, it remained there until it was reallocated to Newton Abbot in 1967, followed by withdrawal and scrapping in 1972.

On the right is North British Type 2 diesel-hydraulic No D6304 (identified from another photo taken from a different angle). These engines were built in 1959-62, and most were initially allocated to Laira. This example spent its entire short life here, entering traffic in June 1959 and lasting until May 1968.

XP

In early 1962 Lance was at Hull Inwards Yard for a demonstration by Dowty of the company's wagon control system. This had been under development since 1958, and eventually trial installations were made at yards in Hull and Goodmayes, Essex. The equipment consisted of three types of 'hydraulic displacement devices' fixed to the track – retarders, retarder boosters and arresters – used separately or in combination. In appearance they were like 'hammer heads', protruding above the inside of each running rail so as to strike the flanges of passing wagons. Each 'hammer' was attached to a piston, actuated by the wheels' pressure on the 'hammer head'. If a wagon (four-wheeled or bogie) passed at too high a speed, it depressed the piston rapidly, increasing the internal pressure and operating a speed control mechanism; the opposite was true of a wagon travelling too slowly. The retarder booster was connected to a hydraulic power supply through pipes laid down the centre of the track. This slowed or accelerated a wagon, but power could be cut to allow vehicles to run over the 'hammers' without activating them. Of this trial, 'Modern Railways' reported that it 'was fascinating to watch a succession of cuts … propelled over the hump and then see them follow each other at a steady 3mph down the reception siding, the interval between the cuts never varying.' The system was different from the 'clasp retarders' already encountered at Margam (see page 30).

As a result of the successful installation in plain line in the relatively small yard at Hull, when Tinsley Marshalling Yard opened in 1965 it was the first in the world to be equipped with the Dowty system. Each of the main sorting sidings was fitted with these computer-controlled devices, but the system was very complex and needed almost constant maintenance, with leakage of oil being one of the problems.

Also being demonstrated at Hull on that day, using the same rake of wagons, was the Dowty Automatic Coupler. This was a side-retraction coupler, which, when retracted, allowed normal drawhooks to be used. It had various disadvantages, however; when reversing, conventional buffing gear still had to be used, so there was no weight saving, and lack of compatibility with other forms of automatic coupling and conventional drawhooks would have required the coupling always to be retractable.

Opposite: The winter of 1962-63, known as the 'Big Freeze', is well documented as one of the coldest on record in the UK. It began with overnight blizzards at the end of December 1962 and continued without respite until the beginning of the following March; the 6th of that month was the first morning without a frost. Gradually the snow disappeared, and the slow thaw meant that widespread flooding was avoided.

This picture was taken some time in March and shows Patchway Tunnels, between Stoke Gifford and the Severn Tunnel, with snow still laying. This is the view looking south-east in the direction of Bristol. The original tunnel here is that on the right, at the higher level; it was one of two, 62 and 1,246 yards long. Before the Severn Tunnel was opened this was a single line to the cross-river ferry at New Passage Pier. When the Severn Tunnel opened it was decided to double the track, but the original line rose from the Severn towards Patchway at a gradient as steep as 1 in 68, which was considered too steep, especially for heavy coal trains. The new, second line, 3 miles long, was therefore built at a gentler gradient of 1 in 100, and its tunnel, 1,760 yards long, was thus at a lower level, seen here (presumably from an approaching train) on the left.

Right: Lance may have been on his way to Rogerston on the Newport-Crumlin line, where this picture was taken. It graphically illustrates one of the problems facing the railway during the 'Big Freeze'. This icy mound is the result of drips falling from the bag of a water column! Behind is a BR English Electric shunter. It could be either No D3816 or D3818 – both were allocated to Newport (Ebbw Junction) at this time.

Winterbourne was east of Patchway, between Stoke Gifford and Westerleigh Junctions. In another 'Big Freeze' view from March 1963, track repairs are being undertaken to part of the crossover in the most inclement of conditions. We are looking east, with the signal box on the right and the station and footbridge beyond the bridge; immediately beyond the station is Huckford Viaduct, carrying the line over the River Frome. On the left is the goods yard; the cattle pen siding is occupied by what appear to be some snowed-in 'Lowmac' (Low Machine) wagons, and a mineral wagon. Behind the camera on the left were a couple of further sidings and a goods shed. The station had been opened on the GWR's 'South Wales and Bristol Direct' line in 1903, but had a relatively short life. By the date of this picture it had been closed to passengers since April 1961, and closed entirely in October 1963.

The steam shed at Swansea Landore was built by the GWR in 1932, and closed in June 1961. It was replaced on the same site by a purpose-built diesel depot in 1963, so when this photograph was taken in March or April of that year it must have been very new. Hardly less new is shiny maroon-livered 'Western' diesel-hydraulic No D1050 'Western Ruler', built at Crewe in January 1963. It was allocated to Cardiff Canton, so is presumably here for maintenance – or for display, if this is an official visit. The loco was withdrawn in April 1975 after clocking up 1,176,000 miles, and was scrapped 12 months later at Swindon. Landore depot itself closed in December 2018, having latterly serviced the GWR's fleet of InterCity 125s, but the site reopened the following year as a rolling-stock refurbishment centre.

Left: Two iconic bridges stand side by side spanning the River Tamar between Plymouth and Saltash, joining Devon with Cornwall. The first, seen on the right in this early 1963 picture, is Brunel's Royal Albert Bridge, carrying the single line of the Cornwall Railway, later part of the GWR, into that county. It consists of two 455-foot (138.7-metre) 'lenticular' (lentil-shaped, or biconvex) iron trusses 100 feet above the water, with conventional plate-girder approach spans. The finished bridge was opened by Prince Albert on 2 May 1859. Ill-health prevented Brunel from attending, and he died later that year. As a result the Cornwall Railway made the bridge its designer's memorial by adding 'I. K. BRUNEL, ENGINEER, 1859' in large metal letters on the portals at both ends.

Just over a century later the Tamar suspension bridge was completed alongside, carrying the A38 road, and providing a stark contrast to Brunel's structure. At 335 metres (1,099 feet) long, it was begun in 1959, unofficially opened in October 1961, and formally opened by the Queen Mother in April 1962. The initial toll for cars was 3 shillings single or 4s 6d return, about the same in real terms today (£2.60 single). Seen beyond the steamer passing upstream is Ernesettle Jetty, which was used to take munitions by lighter down to naval vessels moored lower down the river.

Above: A broader view of the two bridges, looking upstream, possibly from a train heading south from Saltash station.

TRAILING END

This is Camelford station on the North Cornwall line, probably in April 1963. Historically a London & South Western Railway line, it became part of the Southern Region on nationalisation in 1948, but soon afterwards, on 1 July 1950, together with all SR lines west of Cowley Bridge Junction, Exeter, it was transferred to the Western Region. Then, from 1 January 1958, the route was transferred back to the SR until 1 January 1963 when, in another reversal of policy, the whole of the SR west of Salisbury returned to WR control! The line's fortunes gradually went into steep decline, and the whole route from Meldon Junction to Wadebridge finally closed on 3 October 1966.

In 1963, therefore, the route was newly back under Western control, hence Lance's visit in the Plymouth Divisional Engineer's Inspection Saloon. This splendid vehicle was itself on borrowed time, which is probably why Lance captured this picture. GWR Clerestory Family Saloon No 249 had been built in 1894, and had the unusual 'royal clerestory roof', with its characteristic domed end overhanging the body. It was designed by William Dean, with a sumptuous interior, which included a drawing room, private compartment and kitchen. It was rebuilt as the Divisional Engineer's Saloon in 1940, and withdrawn in 1963.

Two years later it was privately preserved, and retains many original features, as can be seen today at its present home on the South Devon Railway.

The locomotive in charge is North British Type 2 diesel-hydraulic No D6325 of 1960, Laira-based at this time. Its short life ended in October 1968, and it was scrapped by Cashmore of Newport the following spring.

1967-68

Although the bulk of the photographs included in this book were take between 1959 and 1963, there are also a few interesting ones taken during 1967 and 1968, so this 'bonus chapter' will include a few of them.

A BR(W) notice issued in August 1967 stated: 'From 15 October to 19 November 1967 the Chief Civil Engineer will be engaged in remodelling the track layout between Paddington and Westbourne Park (Subway Junction)' to install 'Multiple Aspect Colour Light Signalling all of which will be controlled from a new panel at Old Oak Common Signal Box.' Old Oak Common to Subway Junction had been dealt with by the middle of September, with Subway Junction to Paddington during the following two months.

The work is under way here, looking towards the Paddington terminus beneath the 1909 Westbourne Bridge. The casually dressed men appear to be bolting down some new track, and only the Look Out men, with their flags, wear what then passed as 'high-visibility' jackets – and not a hard hat to be seen!

In the background are wagons in the sidings outside the huge Paddington goods station.

Half a mile or so further down the line is Subway Junction, seen here on the same day, looking west. The signal box can be seen in the distance beyond the footbridge that connected Hampden Street on the right (long since subsumed beneath the Westway), and Westbourne Park Villas on the left.

The 'subway' itself was the short tunnel that took the Metropolitan's Hammersmith & City Line beneath the GW main line to head south towards Ladbroke Grove. The railings at the edge of the cutting can be glimpsed behind the lookout man on the right, who is standing in what would become the Up Relief Line in the new layout. Behind him is the Down Relief 2 and in front of him Down Relief 1, then, after the lifted track, the Up and Down Main lines.

Left: Subway Junction signal box opened in September 1911 and was closed on 19 November 1967, the presumed date of this photograph, as S&T staff are busy removing equipment from the block shelf. The track diagram appears to be still in situ, top right. A sad scene of dilapidation.

Opposite: This and the photograph on page 94 of Paddington station appear to have been taken from the Station Master's (or Directors') balcony, which projects from the first floor of the range of office buildings along Platform 1. The window and balcony, still to be seen, were designed by architect Matthew Digby Wyatt as a triple oriel with arched openings and Moorish-style ironwork.

REFRESHMENTS
LICENSED BAR
TICKET OFFICE
SUBWAY
SUBWAY

The second view is looking towards the station concourse, always known as the 'Lawn', as it was originally built on land that contained a number of cottages and their gardens. Standing in Platforms 1 and 2 are unidentified 'Western' diesel-hydraulics, both in maroon, while in Platform 3 is one of the WR's 'Blue Pullmans'. The date on the slide mount indicates that the date is some time in June or July 1968.

INDEX

Follow the Western Region, then you will like these:

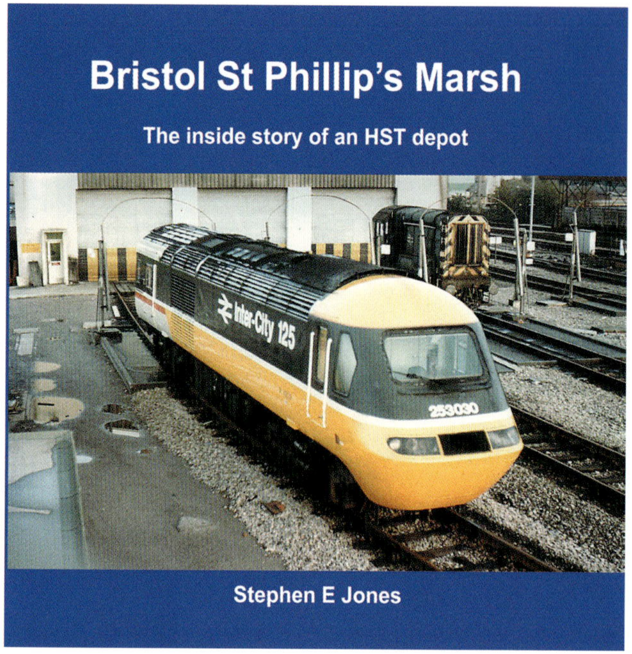

Published by and available from The Transport Treasury